17515

D1011245

Library
Oakland S.U.M.

Library
Oakland S.U.M.

248.43
Edw

THE GIFT OF WHOLENESS
Hal L. Edwards
Foreword by Keith Miller

Word Books, Publisher
Waco, Texas

THE GIFT OF WHOLENESS

Copyright © 1975 by Hal Edwards. All rights reserved. No part of this book may be reproduced in any form, except for brief quotations in reviews, without the written permission of the publisher.

Printed in the United States of America.

Library of Congress catalog card number: 74-27479

1523

To Betsy:

> the girl I ran against for vice-president
>   of the freshman class in college;
> the girl who told me that roses turn black
>   if you force the petals open;
> the girl who screamed for both of us
>   when I was too closed up to know the score;
> the girl who keeps on living it out with me.

Contents

Contents

Foreword

Hal Edwards has written a clear and honest account of a very human journey toward personal wholeness. As a man and as a Christian minister he takes us with him on trails which are sometimes strangely familiar as we see behaviors, feelings, and ideas about life which have frightened, angered, or delighted us on our own private journeys. Hal is honest in indicating the parts of his religious heritage which he finds to be helpful and real and those which he has discovered are, for him only excess baggage on the road toward Christian wholeness.

This is not a book of abstractions but directly presents a living experience still in process. Having been both an observer and participant in some of the events described, I can vouch for their authenticity. The book is written with a clear and readable style. But more important for the reader, I think that Hal and Betsy are trying to discover and live out the implications of "relational Christianity" with a special kind of commitment and integrity, the very existence of which gives me hope for renewal in the church.

Whether you are a Christian parent wondering what your hangups are doing to your children, or a person wrestling with his or her vocation or direction as a minister, there will very likely be something in this book for you. However, I think the primary contribution the author makes is to describe realistically the fear and resistance to personal vulnerability which any minister or lay person must face if he hopes realistically to have his life or church become a center for Christian growth toward wholeness.

If you do not know Hal Edwards, it is with real pleasure that I participate in introducing him to you as a good friend and fellow struggler. One of his former parishioners once said to God in a prayer: "Hal let us see him as he really is, and in seeing him we've found You." I hope this may be the experience of many of you as you read this book.

KEITH MILLER
Port Aransas, Texas

Preface

This is a story of the love-shapers of my past—how my search for personal wholeness and sanity invited me into a new self-image; indeed, a new relationship with God and the church.

I am now freer than before to own my past. I can't forget it or leave it back there. I have to ask myself the questions no one else can ask me, and I've searched all my life for certain people—people who by the goodness of God's compassion could help me unlock a few boxes.

Be prepared to open a few boxes in the attic of your own psyche . . . boxes that may be covered with dust and cobwebs and packed away for a long long time, while, at the same time, ever present because of their power to affect current attitudes, behavior, and values.

I invite you to deal with *your* story, *your* search for wholeness, *your* surprises and discoveries. I can only tell you my story. I have no answers for you. But perhaps my story will awaken a few memories in your own past and, by sharing them in a community of caring people, you too may find encouragement toward wholeness. It can happen! That's what God is all about!

—HAL EDWARDS

Acknowledgments

I wish to express appreciation and thanks to Barbara Kane and Marie Holub who typed the manuscript; to Dean and Lois Griffith who have provided a place and the affirmation; to those CLC K-Groups who have spent so much time and energy sharing parts of the manuscript; to Ron Patterson and Floyd Thatcher who have been very helpful editors; to Keith Miller who has stayed with me and encouraged me, who has ministered to me personally; to Char Meredith and Bruce Larson who have given me assistance with the manuscript; to our children—Libby, Rachel, Sam, and Joanna who encouraged me to keep at it when I just didn't feel like writing; to the beautifully human people who appear in this book—people who have helped me unlock a few of my tight boxes.

To Ron Rusling whose gift of illustration represents a great perception into all our lives.

Thank you, each of you, for enabling me. I feel as though we are a community of authors, and this book owes its existence to all of us.

Searching

Searching, by it's own nature,
    doesn't own a title during it's own time.
Searching is naming the pieces that fall or fit—
    one by one.
Searching is painful—and risky.
Searching—that's the story of many years—
    years that finally spell
    Me
    God
    You
    Life
    History
    Others
My searching is unique,
    as your search is unique.
And it now makes sense—
    Afterwards.
Had I chosen not to search
    I should never have discovered
    The Gift of God
    in me, for me,
    around me.
Search, dear soul, for your Source.
    He will not leave you alone
    until your searching becomes celebration!
                   —Hal Edwards

1
Me?
A Person
of Promise?

1. Are you ready to receive and celebrate your uniqueness as a person?
2. Was it easy or difficult to receive approval and acceptance when you were a youngster? Why?
3. How does your image of God and Jesus fit into your personal search for wholeness?
4. When do you first recall dealing with the question, "Am I a person of promise, a person with tremendous potential?"

PROPERTY OF
LIVING FAITH CENTER
LIBRARY
SANTA BARBARA, CA.

1

Me? A Person of Promise?

Psalm 127:3—*Each of us is God's gift.*
Romans 4:17; 5:1–2—*You are a person of promise!*
1 Peter 1:8–9—*Your trust in God enables wholeness.*
Hebrews 11:1—*Something very special can happen to you.*

It all started in my family's chicken yard. My search for wholeness began here because this was one of my favorite places during childhood. You would never know that it was there now, but thirty years ago we had our own private zoo. Chickens—red ones, speckled ones—ducks, guineas, hogs, an old mule, and dogs of all shapes and descriptions made this place a child's fantasy land.

We also had two old horse stables, a corn shed, and a two-story packhouse. In the corn shed I searched through strange corners to find all kinds of exciting things—most of them covered with rust. An old drawing knife stashed away for many years before I claimed it became my favorite tool.

My chores included feeding the chickens, cutting splinters, bringing in the coal or kerosene, sweeping the yards, and hoeing crabgrass in the garden behind the packhouse. Chore time provided me a real opportunity to listen to my own thoughts and daydream a lot.

Once when I was about ten, I was in the process of throwing corn out to the chickens and I suddenly thought to myself, "There's something gnawing inside of me that's got to come out." A quiet feeling . . . something very real, surged inside of me. It may have been my imagination, or the projection of something someone had previously said. No matter. I'm convinced now, thirty years later, that

18

something special *did* happen. I didn't know it then, but as I look back, I find great meaning in that event. I've thought about that moment many times. A small quiet voice seemed to say, "You are unique, too. Your life *will* be special. I will show you how to love yourself so you can also help people love each other."

For years I buried those feelings. I was afraid that people would think I was weird. Once I heard my Sunday school teacher tell the story of Joseph and how he dreamed that God was going to bless him, and how his brothers became angry and threw him into the deep pit. I discounted my own particular experience—or tried to— but it kept coming back and I couldn't forget it.

Actually, I didn't feel comfortable with such a gift. I couldn't understand that God continually communicates equally important messages to everyone else. I thought if I were to be happy I would have to earn my acceptance, work hard at being responsible—like doing my chores, studying hard, and minding my parents. My childhood feelings told me that in order to be *all right* as a person, I needed to work hard at it so that one day I'd grow up and be an adult and then *something* would happen to me. I didn't know it was okay to feel good about being uniquely myself during those younger years.

I am convinced that each of us has something special going. We have our own uniqueness. We have our special memories (whether we can consciously call them forth or not)—memories filled with joy, happiness, pain, loneliness, rejection, and a thousand other emotions. Each of us has a meaningful past.

To encounter affirmation from God, no matter how, where, when, or why it gets through to us, is to experience another piece of wholeness. He does come to each of us personally. He may also show up in the colors of a sunset, or in the silence of a dark quiet room, or in a book, or in the daily push at the office. He constantly hounds us with affirmation. He continually encounters us, moment by moment, with himself. He has come to us; he is with us in Person and in daily personal relationships! He often comes through other persons—sometimes through the most unlikely ones!

Sometimes we misread his signals. Sometimes we see his gifts and draw back out of fear—the fear of failure, or the fear of being embarrassed by others knowing about a particular failure.

One of the greatest things I'm discovering is that I've often misread his signals. My fear or misguided sense of self-worth, my feelings of ungiftedness, or un-uniqueness, often block his affirmation that comes from many places. During those moments I am denying his grace and personal investment in my humanness.

God has broken through to me often enough to help me begin to understand and experience the constancy of his grace. I'm now more able to celebrate my own feelings of self-worth and his investment in me—*in each of us*. I've come to accept myself as *a person of promise*. I now know that this ability to accept such healing affirmation is a gift of God!

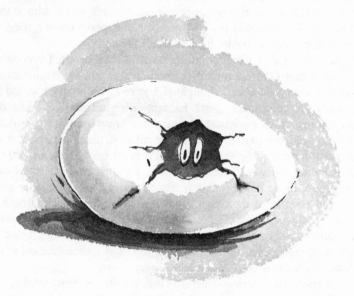

WHAT'S IT LIKE OUT THERE?

I feel like a little chick just popping out of his shell. It's very exciting to peek through into a new world—a world much bigger and more colorful than I ever dreamed. For a long time I've felt like an isolated lonely person trying desperately to love others and not succeeding because my shell was so very thick. It takes a long time to crack it enough to get a good peek at the new world—God's world of affirmation and reality. Keith Miller says we can "create an atmosphere of safety and warmth (through confession) in which the chicken can come out from the inside at his own speed."

There are a few beautiful people-warmers who have affirmed me into the kingdom. It wasn't their answers particularly; rather, it was the shape of their relationships, attitudes, and honesty. Once I heard what was really going on inside these people I felt a new motivation to break loose too.

"Is there really a person of promise inside me?" I've asked myself many times. "How does God fit into my search for promise?" was the question which would not let me go.

Obviously, I'm still trying to crack out of my shell. But at least I'm in the chicken yard and it's fun to know that I belong to others who are in various stages of cracking through their shells, too.

There are many unborn promises residing in each of us and the most exciting thing in the world is to be in a new place of birth, hear a new insight, or see an authentic relationship develop. I feel like God has given some of us the joyful, painful privilege of being cheerleaders for each other. As we encourage each other along in Jesus Christ we will also, to some degree, incarnate the warmth of God's living Presence. Certainly we are *people of promise.*

I want to hold hands with those who desire to burst out of their shells. I want to share what it means, for me, to chip away at it. It's my hope that you and some other people will set up little nest-places where you too can warm each other's lives into wholeness. I hope that my personal illustrations help you find the courage and imagination to share more of yourself with a group or personal friend.

WHERE DO I GO FROM HERE?

Remember the story of Isaac's birth? He was born to Abraham and Sarah (Genesis, chapters 22 to 27). God gave both parents new names and he promised them great blessings. Abraham and Sarah experimented in faith together; they even abused the affirmation God gave, and finally they owned their gifts. And then Isaac, child of promise, was born.

What God was accomplishing in these people he wants to accomplish in each of our lives. There's an Isaac, a person of great promise, to be born in you and me!

Welcome, fellow person of promise! Let's share and grow together and see what the future holds for each of us!

Lord, you mean I can change? I want to experience and feel hope stirring within me. I identify with others who really want to burst out of their boxes.

Help me listen very carefully to the inner signs of a new awareness. Give me the sensitivity and wisdom necessary to find my hitching post.

I'm a person-of-promise, Lord. I am. You've made it possible for me. I claim my birthright by grace. I receive my Isaac-hood.

Where do I go from here? Will you show me . . . one step at a time? I'm a first-grader in the School of Wholeness. But I'm ready to grow, to learn, to stretch and even hurt if need be. . . .

I'm going to begin growing right here. I don't have to be somewhere else, or be somebody else. I'm ready to be uniquely myself and let you into the past, present, and future of my uniqueness!

2

I Looked Like
a Good
Little Boy

1. What feelings did you deny in childhood: sexual feelings, anger, guilt, fear, loneliness, joy, curiosity, relaxation? Why?
2. Is it "Christian" to be angry . . . to express anger? What happens to you when you repress those angry feelings? What happens when you express them?
3. As you read about my axe-event with Todd and Jesse Branch ask what that story says to you. Can you identify at all with it? Where? How? Where are you in that picture? How did you handle anger as a child?
4. Which side of the tracks did you grow up on? How do you feel now about your childhood identity? Is that important to you? Why? Why not?
5. How do you relate to Santayana's quote: "Those who cannot remember the past are condemned to repeat it?"

2

I Looked Like a Good Little Boy

Psalm 55:1-8—*Do you ever tell God about your fear and anger?*
Hebrews 12:14-15—*How can we deal with our negative feelings?*
James 5:16—*Does God want us to admit our faults? To whom?*
James 2:1—*Who's ahead in the growth-game?*

I was a very sensitive and observing child. However, I oftentimes *felt* alone and very small. My parents tell me I was a happy and helpful child. I looked that way to them, and, in truth I may have been.

There are at least three tracks of information relating to my childhood. There is (1) *what I remember feeling;* (2) *what other people remember;* and (3) *what actually did happen,* which may be altogether different from what I remember! What I "think" happened may have had more of an impact on my life than what *actually* happened. In either case, the emotional facts established in my personal memory bank are tremendously important. That emotional past is still a controlling factor in my present behavior and style of communication.

To this day I retain a habit from childhood that really bugs me. I've been biting my nails all my life. I could never remember when or how I started so I decided to talk about it with my parents. At first I was afraid to ask them about this particular habit. I was afraid they wouldn't remember or be interested. I was wrong.

"You were about six," my mother said, "and we were at the doctor's office. You had to have your jaw teeth pulled and our family doctor and I were setting up an appointment with a dentist. He suggested that you be put to sleep with ether. While we were making arrangements, you disappeared. We searched through the offices, the

24

waiting rooms, the hallway, the rest rooms, and finally Dr. Watson found you hiding behind a door. When he saw you, you looked up at him and said, 'Dr. Watson, don't give me that ugly tasting ether. [I had had a previous operation for which they had given me ether. I was sick at my stomach for days. I hated the stuff!] I'm a big boy. Promise me you'll not give me ether.' Dr. Watson promised. Your jaw teeth were pulled without ether, and you've been biting your nails ever since."

I'M SCARED

I'd like to pin my nail-biting on that one particular incident, but I'm afraid it would be unrealistic. However, it is a symbol of the kind of quiet, hidden anxiety I felt in my early childhood. I've often found myself wanting to be a big man—whatever being a big man meant. I thought it meant not feeling weak and scared. The gap between what I felt inside and what I thought I ought to be and feel created tension. I suppose nail-biting was one way I acted that tension out.

Feelings of being afraid, being small, of hurts and hates, and feelings of guilt were deep inside of me, and I didn't want them to be there. I tried all kinds of ways to lock them out, push them down, deny them, and counteract them with good behavior. I had no idea that I was denying my own identity by refusing to allow these feelings out into the open. How was I to know at such an early age that feelings don't die, they just hide away until they finally express themselves in baffling symbolic ways!

I remember Bonnie, a black man, who came to work for us. He plowed the garden and cut huge pine slabs into smaller pieces so we could make kindling for the coal-burning stoves throughout the house. Bonnie was a strong man. In the summertime he'd take his shirt off and his big muscles, covered with sweat, sparkled in the North Carolina sunshine. He kept the heavy axe sharp, and all the children knew that it was a forbidden object.

HOW FAR DO I GO TO BE ME?

One day I was playing in the backyard with two of my best friends, Todd and Jesse Branch. I was five. Todd was teasing me about something and I got so mad I told him I'd . . . I'd go get the wood axe and hit him on the head if he teased me one more time. Well, Todd kept teasing me and I strutted over to the garage and dragged the axe back to the scene. I made up my mind I'd stand up to him and act "like a man." The more I played big, the more it attracted excitement from my other friend, Jesse. He'd never seen me get angry like this before. My pride was at stake as I stood between my best buddies. Todd was daring me to hit him and Jesse was dancing up and down with excitement. He kept "egging me on" until finally I let go. Somehow, that heavy axe went up into the air and came down right on Todd's head! *Blade first!*

The next thing I knew, blood was gushing out and Jesse was running home. Mothers came running from everywhere and Todd was rushed to the hospital. I felt totally rejected by everyone. The whole world had tumbled in on me. I knew I had utterly betrayed my friend. My anger violated what my parents, grandparents, and Sunday school teachers had taught me all my life. I just *knew* that I shouldn't have expressed feelings of anger. "Look what happened," I thought to myself. I was scared. My friend lay bleeding and probably dying in a hospital. That settled it. "I will not let myself get angry again," I told myself.

I was telling this story sometime ago at a conference and after my talk a young man came up to me. He grabbed me and hugged me. "Hal, your story is almost identical to mine. I was fourteen when I hit my best friend. The only difference is that my friend died and I've been in the penitentiary for twenty-five years."

It dawned on me that I was just one-eighth of an inch away from being a five-year-old murderer. I simply didn't know how to express my anger—so I projected it nonverbally!

Thank God, Todd lived through it and we were the best of friends all through school. We played football, basketball, baseball, and shared many hours together through the years. Today he is still my friend, and, needless to say, I am the recipient of his undeserved acceptance! To know that Todd forgave me and accepts me is one more sign of God's affirmation in my past!

I grew up thinking that I was on the side of the good guys. There was this big kid in our third grade class. He had flunked the first and second grades and was a good foot and a half taller than any of us.

Elmer, I figured, wasn't as good as I. I belonged to a neat family, went to Sunday school and had lots of attendance pins to prove it! I made all A's, had nice clean clothes . . . and I thought this made me better than Elmer. Elmer nearly always wore the same overalls to school—and high top shoes without socks. I thought that was awful.

One day I teased Elmer about being so dumb and dirty. I talked down to him. Finally he simply had enough. After school he chased me into an empty lot and beat the devil out of me. I didn't know how to fight so I just screamed for help. Elmer was so mad he stuck weeds into my eyes and then tried to gouge them out. A woman happened to come by and used a stick to chase Elmer away. I was humiliated to discover that I did not know how to fight. I went home and tried to explain away the situation by putting a good face on my side of the argument. I said, "Elmer tried to put my eyes out, but I didn't fight back . . . honest. You can ask Mrs. Brown. She hit Elmer with a stick."

My mother was wise enough to read through my phony report. She reminded me that I deserved just what I got from Elmer. I didn't know how deeply I had hurt Elmer with my self-righteous snobbery.

Many years later I learned that Elmer went to prison and died. I was one of many who didn't know how to communicate affirmation to Elmer. My inner conflict and fear caused me a great deal of anxiety and I know this is not unrelated to my nail-biting. On the outside I acted and appeared to be superior; on the inside I was biting myself—totally afraid. I'm still trying to work through this one.

I often wondered why I felt so mixed up. What did it mean to be a big grown-up person? During my entire childhood I thought I was meant to wait until adulthood to feel put together. I thought adults, especially my parents and grandparents, had it all together. Once I then I'd have it made!
became a real man, I thought, like Tarzan, Gene Autry, or Dad,

I like Santayana's words about the past: "Those who cannot remember the past are condemned to repeat it."

The fact is I do want to learn from my past. Most of us want to, even though it makes us uncomfortable at first.

I'm ready to remember and grow and change *as much as I can. Even* if it means some pain. I want to introduce more healing to the little boy way down deep inside. I've learned that when I share something of my personal life with people who listen and care, a healing takes place. Especially with people who celebrate the living Presence of God in the normal "unreligious" action of daily communication. This kind of communication may not sound religious at all. In fact, it is too simple and realistic to sound "religious."

WHAT DO I DO WITH THIS WORLD?

I have a desire to know as much as I can about who I was, how I felt, how I came across to others during my early childhood. I can learn a lot from the little child in my past. I know one thing for sure —that little boy back there isn't too different from the man I see in the mirror today. Not very different at all. Perhaps the miracle is that I'm beginning to enjoy him. I also notice how I love myself— in new ways.

Lord, I'm not my mask. You know that . . . I know you do. And I also know you see underneath to my real feelings . . . feelings I am unable to admit to myself at times. That's why I clog up in many of my prayers to you. I simply don't know myself that honestly.

Somebody said "feelings aren't good or bad. They just are." If that's true (and I believe that it's true), then you can help me.

Show me how to express my feelings creatively and honestly, and then help me surrender them to you and put them to work in helpful ways. Teach me how, when, and where to deal with those deeper more intimate parts of my inner life.

Somehow I yearn to experience the sacredness of emotional healing. Is that possible for me, Lord?

3

Switches,
Popcorn,
and Chewing Tobacco

1. Did you grow up in a prejudiced racial structure? How did you deal with your racial prejudice during childhood? Are you consciously aware of having experienced any racial prejudice?
2. Which parent seemed closer to you? Why? When, if ever, do you remember being affirmed by one or both of your parents? What did that mean to you then? What happened as a result of their affirmation?
3. Did you enjoy a world of fantasy and excitement in your childhood? Who were your childhood heroes?
4. Who are the important adults in your childhood? Why are they important? How do you feel about each of the specific ones that come to you as you look back in your memory?

3

Switches, Popcorn, and Chewing Tobacco

Ephesians 6:1–4—*Why are obedience and mutual respect essential for parent-child communications?*
James 1:6–7—*Did you get what you asked for as a child? Why?*
Psalm 139:13–18—*Have you discovered that God is intimately involved in the delicate parts of your life?*
Matthew 10:39—*Why not trust God with your most intimate relationships?*

Jesse and I were always into something. We made some mud pies one day and planned to throw them over the front fence. We felt secure and well hidden and the thought of plopping a mud pie on somebody's head just thrilled us no end. I threw mine first. It zoomed over the fence toward the sound of an approaching unseen target. Zip—*wham!* It hit somebody all right and that person turned out to be Deecie, the black lady who had taken care of me since I was an infant!

Was she ever mad! She chased me around the backyard, over through Mrs. McGlawhorn's garden, back of Jesse's house, all around the chicken yard, in and out of the stables. Every time I turned around she was right there behind me. Finally I climbed up into an apple tree in the backyard, thinking I'd get so high up she couldn't climb up after me. Apple trees, I've learned, aren't *that* high! She stripped off a switch and started whipping my overlapping bottom with great fury. I was thoroughly punished and she painted a red mural on my back side.

"Hal Junior, you get down out of that tree and sit here and listen to me," she said. "How'd you like to have mud pies flung in your face? Ain't you ashamed of yourself? Now you just listen. I've treated you all these years 'jes like one of my own children, and it hurt my feelings when you did that. I'm a somebody too, young man, and never forget that, you hear? You just can't keep on going around treating people like trash. You are bigger than that. You've got more sense than that. Just because I'm black and you're white doesn't mean a thing. Now, you be who you are and stop treating people like that, you hear?"

She swatted me on the bottom and sent me on my way. I was punished and totally accepted, both at once. I realized how cruel and careless I'd been without even thinking. I did feel ashamed, deeply ashamed, and I asked for forgiveness—which was already given with no strings attached. Deecie refused to let me get away with my prejudice—*prejudice I didn't know I had for many years.*

WHY CAN'T WE BE LIKE EACH OTHER?

Actually, I never realized my prejudice until I became a teenager and struggled to know God in a personal way. Somehow I had to deal with my racial prejudice in order to deal realistically with God. Knowing Deecie as a person, as opposed to knowing the blacks as a people, had a tremendous influence on me. I never felt comfortable using the term "nigger" but everyone in my part of the country used it. The term "colored folks" was the best I could do. It wasn't culturally permissible to love Deecie, I know, but I also realize that she was a very significant and wonderful human being in my life. *I was too locked in to love her as an equal.* Neither of us knew what that meant. I'm sure she paid a great price to love me and my three brothers. I abused her time and time again without knowing it, simply because I was part of a prejudiced social structure. I was a problem and I didn't know it! I never fully understood what a WASP was until just a few years ago. Even now I'm not sure what this fully entails. I never dreamed that I was an embodiment of a WASP until I realized the price she and other blacks paid to be my friend.

My dad was the manager of our small town's only movie theater. The Show was the social center of the town when I was a youngster, and I thoroughly enjoyed the unique position of being the oldest son of the theater manager.

I worked off and on at the Show from the time I was in the third grade until I went to college. I sold my first bag of popcorn when I was a second- or third-grader. A man bought a ten-cent bag of corn, handed me a dollar, and I gave him $1.65 change. That was the first experience I remember.

Once again I had the opportunity to communicate with black people. In the south, at that time, black people couldn't sit downstairs with the whites. Some blacks nicknamed the balcony "Nigger Heaven." I boxed up several boxes of corn and a variety of candy bars and walked the balcony aisles. Now these people responded beautifully to a movie. They would really put themselves into it. They'd make a dialogue out of the movies, talking back to the people on the screen. (Bill Cosby's record about Buck Jones' movies is a very realistic projection of my experiences in the balcony.) There was an emotional freedom among these people, and I often had a feeling that I was more at home with myself upstairs than downstairs. Many a night after I cleaned up the popcorn machine I'd sit upstairs and watch the rest of a movie before locking up the place with dad.

I continued to appear like a nice kid on the outside, but inside I was often torn apart. I was always doing what I thought were stupid things and didn't know why. I figured that my dad wouldn't like me if he knew all the dumb things I did. There was no conscious reason why I went into a men's washroom and just started hitting my shoe heel on the drain until it broke through. I knew I was doing wrong but something inside made me do it anyway. I also stole some money from the popcorn machine and bought drinks with it. Once I snatched some nuts from the fruit stand next door and took them home. I cracked and ate them under the bed with the assistance of my new Boy Scout flashlight.

One day dad called me into his office. I knew for sure that he had caught on to something I'd done wrong. But I screwed up my courage and went into his office. "Yessir, ya want me, Dad?" "Yes, I want to tell you something. I've been wanting to tell you this for some time."

I swallowed quietly and acted as if everything were just fine. "I want you to know that I really appreciate having you here with me at the theater. You've been a big help to me. You and your brothers help me a lot, and I love you. I love all my boys."

I walked out of his office wondering what he was up to. Why should my dad tell me that he loved me when all I could think about was broken drains, stolen popcorn money, nuts, and candy bars. It was not until years later that I was able to tell him about these things. I think he knew it all along, or at least I suspected that he knew all about me. One never knows what parents really know—or do not know—about their children.

Papa Will, my dad's father, chewed tobacco. He also enjoyed a cigar after lunch and after supper. He was a little man, about five and a half feet tall, completely bald except for a little white hair around and behind his ears. He didn't hold his shoulders up, and he wore dark blue arm garters to keep those ridiculously long shirt sleeves from draping over his hands. He wore little gold-rimmed glasses. Papa Will often forgot where he left things. Many times I'd let on that I didn't know where his spectacles were, and he'd look all over the house before I'd tell him to put his hand up on his forehead.

He had a fine sense of humor and never missed Sunday school and church. He and the rest of the Edwards family would sit on the same pew—right beside a stained-glass window which opened up at the bottom. Papa would sometimes come to the church with a little chaw of tobacco resting in the back of his jaw. Once, during a pastoral prayer, I saw him spit out through the open window into the bushes. Papa Will almost always fell asleep during the sermon. He'd sit there smiling in his sleep. Now and then his head would nod and his eyes would open. One day we teased him about sleeping during the sermon. "Well, it's like this, you see. I really trust that preacher; that's why I can rest my eyes," he'd chuckle.

Papa Will and Big Mama lived three blocks away from our house. They owned a big house with an upstairs. I thought they were special to have a house with an upstairs. Sometimes I spent a whole day looking through old boxes, trunks, and books stored away in the attic. Sitting in the upstairs junk room flipping through some books one day, I noticed a particular book. In it there were pictures of a baseball player. The baseball player was standing in front of thousands of people with a Bible in his hand. That was a new thought —that baseball players would be interested in God! I loved sports and I went to Sunday school every week but until that day I never put the two together. I was somewhat confused so I went downstairs to the kitchen and called Big Mama. Big Mama was every bit of five feet tall. Her hair was pulled back in a bun. She was making those delicious homemade yeast rolls. She wiped the flour dough off her hands and sat down and listened.

"Sonny Boy [she always called me that], that man's name is Billy Sunday. He loves baseball and he loves God. He's telling all those people that God loves them."

I was too young to understand why her voice would crack and her eyes filled with tears. Years later, after I decided to be a minister she told me how as a child she wanted to be a missionary, but she married Papa Will instead. She felt that she had disobeyed God by not becoming a missionary. She told me about her feelings, and how happy she was that God had called me to be a preacher. It was a surprise to me that she ever wanted to be a missionary. I'll always be grateful for the freedom I felt around her to be whatever I wanted to be.

Back to the book. I listened carefully with wide eyes and returned to the junk room with the open book. I was overwhelmed with the new discovery that God loved me and that baseball players, of all people, would stand up before so many people and talk about God! I was so emotionally captured that tears came and I couldn't understand how I could cry and feel so happy both at the same time. I thought crying happened when people were hurt or sad. That was my first conscious awareness of God's love and my capacity to communicate this love to others.

I'M GOING TO BE LIKE YOU

As I think back, I know I've adopted certain characteristics, attitudes, and values from these and other key people in my childhood. Some of these are quite negative, some are positive. The fact remains, I inherited and created some characteristics because of those people who have influenced me. There's something of Deecie, and mother, dad, Mama Jolly, Papa Will and Big Mama, inside my psyche *today*. I think it's true to some degree that we become like the people who influenced us in childhood.

Because of my relationship with certain adults in my childhood I have developed specific likes and dislikes. I know why I'm quite sensitive to black people—because a woman named Deecie got through to me more than once. I know why I feel good about going to see a movie, any movie, because that's the place where my dad told me he loved me. I sometimes smile when I glance at a broken drain in a public restroom. I still enjoy the therapy of sweeping yards, the smell of fresh pine wood, cleaning dresser drawers, closets, and tool sheds. I find great healing just meandering through hardware stores. I like chocolate cupcakes. These are some positive symbols of significant people and places in my childhood.

These relationships were not always positive. In fact, sometimes I felt very much at odds with some of these people. The overall relationship includes negatives and positives. For years I chose to recall only the hurts and negatives. The older I get the more essential it is to look back and perceive some things with new eyes. I think this is an area in which the Spirit of God works quite regularly, especially through supportive friends.

From time to time we can receive new insights about old experiences and relationships. The more mistakes I make as an adult, the easier it is for me to recompute some past experiences. Now I know, for example, from personal experience of being the father of four children, that even though I love my children, I do not always have the capacity to communicate my love to them. Sometimes I'm so hung up within myself that I simply can't get through to my own family. During those times I'm sure my children question their relationship with me. At least I would *expect* them to feel inadequate or rejected because that's the way I often felt.

Adults have a tremendously powerful influence on little children. Just by being who we are we automatically influence our children and give them raw materials out of which they create their values, attitudes, and life goals. *How frightening! How exciting!* Thank God for his ability to use these relationships for ultimate good! Often I thank him for his tremendous ability to love and guide our children in spite of, and because of, their parents.

Lord, it really shakes me to think about the specific people and places in my past.

Thank you for sending me the people who are teaching me the color of wholeness. Thank you for places where I can cry because I'm happy. Thanks for black people, parents, and grandparents and all of those who loved me when I couldn't express love to them.

Why did I lock myself up so tightly? Why couldn't I see people the way you see them—the way they really are?

How great is your gift—to know your forgiveness for myself, and to express forgiveness for those who aren't able to help me grow.

Thank you for the love-shapers of my past. I'm where I am today because they loved me back there—even and (especially) when I wasn't aware of that costly effort on their part. You were trying to get through to me through them, and I didn't even know it!

4

A Teenager's Search
for Masculinity

1. How would you describe your search for identity during high school?
2. Did you become a campus leader? Why? Why not? How did you gain a sense of accomplishment?
3. What two people (youth or adults) influenced your life most during high school years? How did they influence you?
4. Did you date during high school? Often? Go steady? Go out very little? Why? Why not? How do you feel about it now? How did you feel about it then?

4

A Teenager's Search for Masculinity

Luke 2:31–52—*How does growth demand a new perspective from both children and parents?*
Psalm 130:1–2—*Have you ever cried out to God for help?*
Romans 7:21—*Do you ever feel mixed up with your attitudes and behavior patterns?*
John 14:4–6—*Is there a way that really works in a given situation?*

The Tornado football team was tough again for the third year straight. We were winning our fifteenth consecutive game. I was a freshman and had yet to play during an actual game. The score was 28–0 in our favor and two minutes before the final gun, coach Tripp called my name, "Edwards, go in at left halfback." I was so scared and excited I could hardly put my helmet on, and on the way to the huddle I wondered if I'd forget where the left halfback stood!

I couldn't believe it! I was finally in a *real* game! The football was on the one foot line and our quarterback called a play. I was to run straight into the line and he would lay the ball into my arms. The quarterback called the signals, I bent over and started for the line. Clutching the ball and gritting my teeth I pushed forward, grabbed the ball, pumped my knees, and immediately collapsed underneath a tidal wave of giants. My face was full of lime. I was utterly surprised and elated. The ball was over! Touchdown! Another six points against Zebulon High School!

Making a touchdown, batting out a single to first base, or shooting a freethrow became my rewards during high school. I thought, slept, and daydreamed sports. I dreamed of being All-Conference and was selected to that honor during my junior year. I wanted to play college ball like my dad.

HOW LONG DO I HAVE TO WIN?

My heroes changed from Wild Bill Elliott and Gene Autry to Charlie Justice, Bud Wilkinson, Jim Tatum, and Jackie Robinson. To be a man was to make a touchdown, to help win the game. The attention received from the local townspeople motivated me further. Through athletics I felt a sense of belonging. I worshiped athletics. That was *the one thing I knew I could not give up.* I finally "felt like a man" because I could run, kick, and throw a ball with some degree of precision.

My confidence and interest on the academic side of life was not so high. I made all A's until the seventh grade and then my attention shifted to sports. By the time I was in the tenth grade my motivation to study and complete my homework was quite low. I detested chemistry and algebra; memorizing dates threatened me.

I daydreamed quite often, finding it almost impossible to concentrate on my studies. I couldn't understand why I didn't care about my studies. I felt inferior and didn't like homework. I'd rather practice football, mess around with some friends, or just sit alone on the front porch and rock in my favorite rocking chair. My mom said I was seventh, academically, in my senior class. That sounds like I was a real smart kid until you realize that we had a total of twenty-six graduates in my entire senior class! I constantly underrated myself. That's why I really thought at that time I was about seventh from the bottom!

You see, I had many feelings of inadequacy and this kind of self-image gave me reason to think that I was doing much less than I actually accomplished. As I look back, I see how I accomplished quite a bit, but I didn't see it that way then. I blocked most of the affirmation that came my way. I didn't have enough self-confidence to accept outside affirmation.

THERE MUST BE AN EASIER WAY

Day after day I suffered through an eternity of classes . . . and I'd come alive around 3:18 P.M., my heart set on ball practice. Practice was good therapy. It kept me out of a lot of trouble. There was something very masculine about putting on a uniform. Shoulder pads, knee pads, hip pads, cleats, helmet. Even daily practices, "Okay fellas, get going . . . fifteen laps around the field, get those cobwebs out of your bones!" It felt good to know that I was putting out the very best I had. All my feelings of inadequacy and mixed-upness seemed to go away. Even the homework I had to do after a long day's practice didn't threaten me. I was in the center of pure privilege as I prepared for the next ball game.

A tremendous sense of community developed among the players and coach. We became a body. We understood each other. We were close.

On the outside I looked very happy, outgoing, and competent. People believed in me. I was elected student body president, president of the school chorus, president of the local church youth group, and enjoyed major roles in other school activities. I played first string in all major sports beginning my sophomore year, dated, danced, and attended all the neat parties. I was not only included in the "in" crowd, but helped create the "in" crowd. There were awards in state music festivals, and parts in plays—and I could take a girl to the movies free any time I wanted. My folks owned a brand new "88" Olds and I sported about town with my crew-cut and a Confederate flag tied on the radio aerial.

That's a nifty package for any teenager in a small town in the late forties and early fifties. Everything on the outside looked as healthy and carefree as my rosy cheeks. The truth is, I was very lonely and anxious and no matter how much I seemed to accomplish, it did not fill the inner vacuum. Oh, I did enjoy the taste of victory; I got a lot of attention when I scored or made a good tackle. But always my self-acceptance was built on some accomplishment or achievement.

To accept myself without earning a neat award was totally foreign to my way of living.

My search for value, significance, and belonging as a young adult was often very painful. I experimented with many different things and was open for new friendships. I was ready for something. My pastor, Reverend Fogleman, must have sensed this.

Jack Fogleman was different. Most of the other preachers who came to our church were too religious or something. Jack attended ball games and he didn't try to change me. He even let me listen to rock and roll music on his car radio. He liked to travel and often took me with him. He was a good listener. There was a warmth and a feeling of availability about him. He invited me to the parsonage. I'd seldom visited a preacher in his home. I mean, just to be with the preacher as a friend. We'd sit and talk and joke around. When Jack spoke during the worship on Sunday I felt things clicking together inside of me. I sometimes felt put together and close to God after hearing him preach. I didn't know why or how this happened, but I began to trust him. This was the beginning of a new type of friendship. Somehow, when I was with Jack, God became more real. This was new for me.

We spent a lot of time together. The way he listened helped unravel the different me's inside. There was the *athletic* me, the *humorous* me, the *insecure* me, the *spiritual* me.

I wanted to let Jack know me, and, at the same time, I was afraid to let him in. Gradually, after a few months, the wished-for opportunity came. We were alone, and I started talking about my sexual feelings. Feelings about sex is a dangerous subject for a teenager to bring up with an adult—at least, I thought so then. I told him some things, shared some of my fantasies, and then held my breath. "My God!" I thought, "I've blown it for good now!"

Instead, he surprised me. He wasn't shocked with my sexual feelings; in fact, he told me about his. I was amazed to hear an adult talk about himself so freely. It was absolutely freeing. His gentle and normal acceptance of me, including my feelings about a very vulnerable subject, affirmed me deeply. I trusted him and he handled it beautifully! Jack loved me, and this enabled me to trust more in God. Sunday worship didn't seem like church anymore; it seemed like everything was new. I *wanted* to go.

During my sophomore year I double-dated with guys two years older than myself. One night I was dating a cute gal and my buddy was riding in the back seat with his girlfriend. We went to a drive-in movie and I noticed his girl in the front seat. She was really different. On our way home I discovered that my friend was breaking up with her so I asked Ann for a date.

For the first time in my life I communicated authentic personal feelings with someone my own age. She *wasn't* like the other girls. She *was* different. We both enjoyed dancing, and we talked for hours about things that made life interesting, fun, and exciting. We dated for three years. Both of us were very much in love and we talked of marriage after we graduated from college.

Something happened between my senior year of high school and freshman year of college which deeply affected our relationship. I became *very religious.* Not just Christian, but ultra serious and very pious. We both went through months of inner turmoil because we couldn't agree on religious priorities. I stopped dancing. I even stopped going to the movies, and my dad was a theater manager! I became melancholy and depressed. I thought I felt that way because I was doing something against God's will. I attended many Bible-Belt revival services in all kinds of churches. I thought to be a Christian I had to become religious and do *these certain things.* Ann simply could not buy into this religious lifestyle. We broke up and I told her that it was "God's will" that we go our separate ways.

Sixteen years later I had the opportunity to visit Ann again. She married a fine young man and they have a lovely family. I asked her to forgive me for abusing her with my religious ignorance and arrogance. She was very surprised to hear my confession and quite relieved to discover my new freedom and to hear me admit these things about myself. We both were tremendously relieved to talk about it. We set each other free!

Farmville was one of our chief rivals. When we won a game in Farmville, we were extremely happy. It was baseball season and I was a junior in high school. I played catcher and it was my turn at bat. I let the first pitch slide by. It was a ball. The second pitch was just what I wanted and I hit a grounder to the shortstop. Running like crazy to beat the ball to first, I strained as hard as I could and took one long leap. My foot hit the bag and I doubled up with excruciating pain in my left knee. I was carried off the field to a nearby hospital.

The next day my doctor made a surgery appointment at Duke University Hospital. Then came the doctor's stunning remark, "Son, get it straight in your head right now. No more ball playing. Ever. You've just played your last game."

The emotional shock was immediate and absolutely unbearable. I wanted to run away and swear or cry or knock the whole blasted world into shreds! An avalanche of despair smothered me. My mind buzzed with questions and fantasies. "This isn't true. The doctors at Duke will fix me up in no time. Everybody's telling me lies. My mother just doesn't want me to play. I have plans to go ahead and make it through college with a football scholarship. Besides, I'll heal in time for football season next fall. I've got three whole months and I'll show 'em! By golly, I'll show the whole lousy bunch! I'm not going to give up. I'll play again—you wait and see!"

I didn't know how to handle this blow. Big boys weren't supposed to cry, but I found a lonely place and tears of hurt, anger, self-pity, and disbelief flowed.

I talked to Ann. She understood.

A week later I was studying in the library. My friend Betty Jean and I were rummaging through some books about to be thrown away. I was immediately captured by the title of a little volume *How To Find Your Personality*. I needed to know how to find myself, with a bum knee and new questions about my future. I looked through the table of contents. I read a few pages, nothing much inside, but the very *title* of the book was enough for the moment. Somebody else

WHO AM I?

was asking my kind of questions—questions lodged deep in my own personal quest for more! I knew that somehow I'd find *my* personality, if I kept looking long enough. "God," I said quietly as I clutched that book and gazed out the window. "You're going to help me find myself, aren't you?"

I could almost hear him say a faint but clear, "Yes."

It seems to me, Jesus, that you knew yourself as a young teenager. When your mom found you in the temple you didn't sass her, nor did you apologize for being where you felt you should be. You reacted quite spontaneously and owned your behavior.

Being in-between—in those so-called adolescent years—isn't easy in our society. In fact, it's darn hard. Our culture doesn't affirm our identity as persons. Plus the fact that our drives, urges, curiosities and the need to become, to belong, to BE drives us on. Whew! It sure is hard to get through this stage of life.

Jesus, teach me that I am totally loved and uniquely yours at every age. Get it through my thick skull that you really do understand me, even when I am not able to understand myself.

5

One Realistic
Moment
of Love

1. When, if ever, have you experienced a deep and realistic love of God? Is it still meaningful? Why? Why not?
2. Can a so-called tragedy become a tremendous opportunity? Can you speak to this question from your own experience? What specific happening best describes your response to the question?
3. How do you feel about being alone, with time to think and pray? What happens? Think about one specific "time" when you did get off alone with God. Why is that specific time important to you?
4. Have you ever admitted to God that you aren't put together yet, that you're hurting and need help? What did you do about it? What did God do about it? What difference did it make?

5

One Realistic Moment of Love

Psalm 23—*Does God really care about your welfare?*
Romans 8:26–28—*Is it possible that God's Spirit actually loves and prays within us when we reach out to him?*
Psalm 51:7–10—*How does God create what we cannot produce by our own humanity?*
John 15:9—*Can a person build his existence upon God's love?*

Everyone had already dressed for practice so I went into the locker room. I rummaged through the lockers and found enough equipment and headed for the practice field. Knee surgery, performed three months prior, was behind me and I was determined to prove to myself that I could play. I remembered reading the success stories of ball players who were injured and made fantastic comebacks. I wanted more than anything to make a comeback! The teams were scrimmaging. Everyone stopped and looked up in silence, as if to say, "Whatta you trying to prove now, Edwards?"

I didn't ask the coach if I could practice. I was determined to continue until he ran me off the field. The defensive halfback was absent so I slipped into position. My leg felt "great." (I talked myself into making it feel great.) I intercepted a pass and landed a terrific tackle. Then our side got the ball and I threw a long pass. On the next play I took the ball and started running. No one ran after me or tackled me. I knew in a flash that they had decided to let me play, but they wouldn't touch me, much less tackle me, because they didn't want to injure my knee again.

I stopped and looked around at all my buddies, threw the football down, and cursed out of my inner frustrations. No one said a word.

I turned to the gym and walked back alone to the locker room. I slammed my helmet into the locker, kicked, spit, swore, and immediately felt overwhelmed with my inability to cope with the situation.

I dressed and took a walk. Listening to the crunching autumn leaves under my feet, I walked past my house and turned left at the stop light. I walked by the theater. I didn't want to be seen. I didn't want anybody to say anything to me. Two blocks further I came to the church. "I wonder if the key to the sanctuary still hangs over the door that leads to the belfry," I thought to myself. I walked up the steps and looked up over the door. Sure enough, there it was.

I poked it into the sanctuary door. It was dark and very quiet and smelled just like a church. I walked inside and locked the door so no one could sneak in and scare me. Being alone in church sanctuaries was not something I did with a great deal of ease. But this time it seemed different. The stained glass windows were magnificently transforming direct rays of an evening sunset. Everything else was semi-black. I studied the window to the left of the pulpit, the one with Jesus standing by a door. The door didn't have an outside latch. He seemed to be waiting for someone inside to open the door and let him in. When I realized the door had to be opened from the inside I felt a gush of emotion pouring out of me. I wept so hard I thought I'd never quit. I walked up and down the aisles with tears flooding my face. I talked aloud to myself and to God. I let out lots of feelings—how I felt about not being able to play football, how I needed him to help me make a transition. I found myself telling God that I just didn't know how to accept or understand why I couldn't play anymore. I asked him to listen carefully to all my feelings—those I expressed and others I didn't know how to express—and help me deal with them creatively. Before I knew it I was sitting in total darkness, but I didn't feel alone or scared anymore. I sat in silence, relieved. Wonderfully relieved.

The crisp air felt good, and I was glad the key had been hanging over the belfry door. I put it back and started home. From that night on I've made a practice of being alone from time to time with my thoughts in some little sanctuary.

During the summer of my sophomore year I attended a leadership conference at beautiful Lake Junaluska in western North Carolina. On the last night some three hundred of us participated in a very unusual sharing session. The front doors of the lodge opened toward the lake. We all sat in silence. In the midst of the silence

a guy my age stood and shared something personal. I was astonished that kids my age would do something like that. Soon others
stood and spoke from their hearts. Before I knew it I was standing
and my words just flowed out. My heart was beating like a trip
hammer and my hands were wet with perspiration.

The communion table was located between us and the front door.
We were invited to go up and celebrate the Lord's Supper and take
a quiet walk outside. I received the bread and wine and went outside. For a long time I sat in absolute silence. Towering silhouettes of
mountains surrounded me. A huge cross, glowing with light, some
two miles away across the lake, danced across the ripples. Suddenly
I felt quietly consumed with Love. I knew something was happening
to me. A voice, a quiet voice, seemed to say, "You are loved, and
I'll teach you how to love other people the way I'm loving you."

I spontaneously responded, "Yes." I was deeply moved and tears
came. The inner voice said, "Will you do this as a minister?"

I nodded. For quite awhile I walked about the lake. Seldom in my
life have I felt such waves of love consuming me. I knew a revolution
was somehow taking place in my life. It was certainly a realistic moment of love, and in that moment I found myself saying to myself,
"Well, Mr. Edwards, it looks like you're going to be a preacher."

I preached my first sermon in December, 1952. It was twenty-
three and one half minutes long and the title was, "How Many Keys
Do You Have?" I quoted from *Pilgrim's Progress* and *A Man Called
Peter*. I know it wasn't the world's greatest sermon, but the Spirit
of God was very evident in the congregation that morning. A six-year-
old boy who shook my hand at the end of the service said, "Hal,
you know what? I really understood your sermon. You talked so I
could understand everything you said."

I'll never forget those words. Right then I made a vow to keep it
simple and paint plain pictures with my words.

Immediately, however, I noticed a difference in my relationship
with some of my best friends. They didn't curse around me anymore.
They just didn't act like themselves. I felt isolated. I was very excited about what was happening in my life, but I was unable to understand why several of my friends treated me differently—as if being
a clergyman made me something other than myself.

By the time I was a senior in high school my older friends had
graduated and I continued to date Ann (who attended another high
school). I exposed myself to a variety of spiritual experiences. I was
amazed to discover so many avenues open in various churches. I

attended many revival meetings, conferences, and lectures. For the first time in my life I identified with the more conservative groups. I learned that there were different ways to interpret the Bible. I heard about *the* Plan of Salvation. I responded when altar calls were given. I made up my mind to get everything God had for me, no matter what. Without knowing it I became unbearably religious—thinking all the time that my religious activity was Christianity. I confused the two.

The summer of my senior year was spent in New England as a YMCA camp counselor. Fourteen weeks jammed with swimming, softball, overnight hikes, leather-craft classes, and the constant chattering of little voices. It was a great summer. After it was all over, the night before we drove back to North Carolina, I walked down to the lake front. I had the urge to be alone. The loud juke box music from the mess hall disturbed me. I pulled a canoe from the boat rack and pushed it out into the dark calm water. I paddled for half a mile until the silence was broken only by the movement of the paddle. I placed the paddle inside and lay on my back with my hands behind my head. The water was absolutely still. The sky was brilliant with stars. I found myself quoting the Lord's Prayer. Then the Twenty-third Psalm. "God, help me," I prayed. "There's something still mixed up inside of me. I'm not clear about my life. I don't think I'm emotionally put together yet. I'm bumping into myself all the time. God! I'm hurting so much!"

HELP PUT ME TOGETHER AGAIN

I looked up at the stars and continued, "God, will you put things together inside of me? Those stars of yours are moving across the sky with tremendous precision. If you can do that up there, please help things move with greater precision in my heart and mind."

Almost instantly a quietly swishing, cleansing presence happened to me. It was as though God just waited for me to finish talking so he could let me know that he was still alive in my life. Again I wept. I felt his Presence. I didn't talk about this for years. But inside I knew it was for real, and I believed that God was leading me.

I am very confident that years later I would have left the Christian ministry if it had not been for these quiet but very real experiences. There was no flash of lightning, no ringing of bells . . . just a quiet peaceful realization that God was doing something special in me and I could change if I kept responding.

The summer was over and I knew what my life's vocation would be before I started going to college. I returned just in time to pack my trunk and catch a bus for college—seven hundred miles from home.

God, you are love. You do love. You love me. You love us. You love them. Sometimes I can't feel your love. Sometimes I've blocked you out of my picture and I feel void of love. It's for sure I don't understand why or how you keep on loving me, but, oh, I need this depth and quality of undeserved love.

Your love is something else . . . especially when you turn hurt into healing.

I like the way you make coincidences happen without any help from me! You just do it and I see it . . . and it feels like love keeps the whole universe in balance.

When my little world seems rotten you show up and surprise me with another real time of undeserved loving. You really are love, or else you couldn't love me like that. Thank you for that kind of love.

6

Lots of Faith
and
Lots of Feeling

1. Do you ever use the Bible to prove your own point of view? How can you become more accountable in your use of Scripture— particularly when it relates to other people?
2. We all have our unique ways of working out our faith and our feelings. What's the difference between faith and feelings?
3. Have you ever experienced a meaningful time with a dying person? What happened? What did you learn or remember from that experience, or from that particular person?
4. Can you identify any of your past or current religious games? What are you *doing* so that you'll be loved? What's the name of your performance-oriented syndrome?

6

Lots of Faith and Lots of Feeling

Matthew 22:29—*How do Scripture and reality line up together?*
Ephesians 4:25–27—*Do I cheàt myself when I do not deal honestly with my anger? How do I cheat myself?*
Romans 5:1—*How do I get peace with God in my life?*
Ephesians 2:8–10—*How does God's kindness lead you into wholeness?*

During my junior and senior years in high school I had my mind set on attending a well-known university in eastern North Carolina. I applied and received my acceptance. A job and scholarship had been provided. My parents were very happy.

Both my dad and my grandfather had attended this school. My uncle was once a professor there. Everything was settled . . . *except me.*

During this time I received many other college bulletins and brochures. I read and prayed about each of them, really wanting God's guidance. I asked God to help me know where I should go.

One Sunday morning during worship I once again felt that quiet sense of God's presence surrounding me. It was as though an imaginary poster stood before me. The name of one of the colleges, not the university in which I was already preenrolled, became very clear on that imaginary poster. I took that as guidance. As I left the church and shook hands with Jack, my pastor, I said, "I've made a decision, and I'll tell you about it later."

I went home immediately and found the brochure. I went to my room and wrote a personal letter to the dean of the college. "Dear Sir, I know it's very late to try and get into your school for the fall quarter, but (you'll really think I'm crazy now) this morning I think I had guidance from God about this and so I'm asking if by any chance, at this late date, you still can accept my application. I'm very anxious to attend your school, even though I am presently preenrolled in another university. Thank you for responding to my letter as soon as possible."

I mailed that letter within the hour—three months before the fall quarter. I left for New England for fourteen weeks and trusted God for the results. Several weeks later I was granted admission.

Meanwhile, I had an announcement to make to my parents! After I walked to the local post office and dropped my letter in the mailbox, I returned home. "Lord, I really believe this is your guidance, and I need your help. You know how much my parents want me to attend the university. I understand why they'll be upset! They're going to faint when I tell them what I've done. Help me, and *please* help them, too."

I waited until after lunch. Then I told them. Feelings of anger, hurt, and misunderstanding emerged immediately. After the initial blast was over, both parents affirmed my decision, even though none of us knew how we were going to finance such a project.

I felt that God did answer my prayer and the transition was made without a great deal of tension and argument. Looking back, I now know that was a creative decision to make. I didn't know this at that time.

On the bus trip to college I met two North Carolinians who were also going to "my" college. There were never two people in the whole world with such opposite personality traits. Charlie was a comic. He knew a thousand jokes and he must have told them all. He never once stopped talking. And Merlin. Merlin was dressed in black. Black pants, black tie, black shoes, black socks. And, believe me, he wore a black homburg hat. There he sat on one side of me, reading his little Bible, and Charlie was chatting away on the other side. I couldn't identify with either. I was baffled to think that I was going to college for four years with these two fellows. I wondered if I seemed as strange to them as they did to me.

We changed buses in Lexington and enjoyed a short trip through the bluegrass hills of Kentucky. We drove by several beautiful horse farms. I liked the feeling of being in those rolling hills and was glad to be 700 miles away from everything familiar. Even though I did have feelings of insecurity, they were replaced by deeper feelings of expectation.

ARE WE GOING TO THE SAME PLACE?

We got off the bus and I waited for the bus driver to unload my two suitcases and typewriter. My friends went ahead and I walked up to the first dormitory in sight and asked, "How do I find my room?"

An elderly lady without makeup came by and responded, "Well young man, you'll not room here, that's for sure. This is a *girls'* dorm. *Go out* the front door, turn right, and you'll come to the administration building. Go to the registrar's office and they will give you further instructions."

My first college encounter came through like somebody hitting me square in the face with a soggy old dish rag!

Two months later, in October, we had our annual college revival. Great preachers came to the campus each year and preached during chapel every morning and then each evening for two weeks. After each sermon the speaker invited us to come forward and kneel at the altar if we wanted to be converted or filled with the Holy Spirit. I went forward seven nights straight. I tried and tried to "buy in" and get what everyone else seemed to be getting, but I *didn't know how.* People came and prayed with me every night. One person would pray, "Lord, help Hal let go." Someone else would pray "Lord, help this brother hold on."

Another person would pray, "Jesus, reveal to Hal what he's holding back so you can really fill him with the baptism." Another person prayed in great detail, developing a long and involved series of steps called the Plan of Salvation. Sometimes we'd be there for two or three hours at a time. I'd go back to my dorm room exhausted, but I was determined to "get the blessing."

During those four years, I met people who will always be special to me, students and professors alike. The whole college atmosphere was definitely religious. We were standing in the stream of strong tradition. The theology of early Methodism dominated the campus. I was emotionally insecure and often so gullible that I believed anything and everything that *sounded* scriptural. This, I've since learned, is not always healthy! During the course of those four years I had one primary goal—to prepare myself for the Christian ministry. My idea of ministry changed from time to time, especially during my four years in college. When I went to the altar those seven nights in order to find the fullness of God, I recomputed several personal values.

I was taught that to be a Christian I had to "separate myself from the evil in the world."

I could be "*in* the world but not *of* it." That was "interpreted" to mean no more dancing, no more movies, no more ugly thoughts and feelings. I was to give them to God and let him forever cleanse my heart from such things. Then selected scriptural promises were brought to bear upon my case. These specifically chosen verses led me to believe that if I surrendered to God I would be instantaneously and completely sanctified, or cleansed, in my attitudes. This was certainly something I knew I needed—to be cleansed in my deeper feeling level. I knew I felt guilt especially regarding my sexual feelings and feelings of anger. I wanted very much to be cleansed from such "inordinate" feelings. So I prayed that God would sanctify me and cleanse me from all inward and outward sin.

I believed this would happen instantaneously.

I lived with a great deal of guilt because, even though I verbalized all the scriptural doctrine, deep down I felt like a phony. But I couldn't afford to admit it, because everywhere I went I heard others saying these same words. Often I thought I just didn't have what it takes to be a sanctified, Spirit-filled, and baptized Christian. I went into a very deep depression over this and tried to work my way out by becoming *more* responsible, *more* committed, and *more* available to help others for Jesus' sake.

We had no classes after Saturday noon or on Monday. This provided, for many students, the necessary time to travel to their churches and study for the next week of classes. I didn't like to study and found it quite easy to sign up for weekend projects.

Some of the students visited a reformatory, located about twenty miles away. I decided to go with them. The work fascinated me, and I made arrangements to live out there during the summer after my freshman year. Those young inmates taught me so much. I was offered the position of assistant chaplain and recreation director for $30.00 a month plus room and board. I accepted the offer and worked there my first summer in college.

"Killer" McCoy was the name of one of the inmates. He was a tall, black-haired youngster about sixteen years old. He was in for robbery. "Killer" wanted to be the leader, and he talked a lot, but he never quite made it because he was always trying too hard. One day I was teaching some guys how to dive. We were practicing half and full gainers. "Killer" was jealous of the attention the other boys were getting, so he sneaked a folding chair under the diving board when I wasn't looking. It so happened that he forgot he put the chair there and, a few moments later, he tried to show off by doing a crazy dive. He came up out of the water sputtering and cussing a blue streak. He got caught in his own trap.

"Killer" and I spent quite a bit of time together. He came from a broken home and claimed to be a direct descendant of the McCoy family who fought against the Hatfields. He had tattooed his whole chest and stomach with a huge champagne glass with a naked woman sitting in the glass. Just to make sure that nobody missed the point, he had "Killer" tattooed across his stomach under the picture. He was advertising his masculinity—or what he *thought* was masculinity —the best way he knew. I realized he was trying, just like me, to become a man!

My second summer I pastored a storefront church made up mostly of farm families. Then during my last two years in college I served as an assistant pastor and youth minister in a large Methodist church in another Kentucky town. Bill and Betty were laymen in that congregation, and they ministered to me in many practical ways. I commuted to church every Friday night and returned to college every Sunday evening. Bill taught me how to fish and he kept me from being too religious.

By this time there were two Edwards boys in college. My parents consistently sent all they could, and sometimes it wasn't enough. Sometimes there was not enough money to pay the bills. Once I walked into the registration line to sign up for the next quarter. I somehow believed God would provide for me. As I stood in line, wondering what I could say regarding the fact that I didn't have the necessary funds to stay in school, I had another conversation with the Lord. "Lord, I think you called me here. If you don't want me to stay that's okay; but if you do want me to stay, thanks for doing the totally impossible . . . I mean, *right now!"*

Would you believe it? When I asked for my financial balance report, the lady in charge said, "Well, Mr. Edwards, I have good news for you. Someone just paid your next quarter's bill—and he wishes to remain anonymous." I discovered later, months later, that my roommate's father paid that bill! I shall always be grateful for that gift!

I worked in the cafeteria and kitchen for two years and Sunday lunch was the biggest meal of the entire week—turkey, dressing, and all the trimmings. Stacks of plates! Three hours later I'd wash up and go back to my dormitory. On one particular Sunday I promised to visit some people in the slums of Lexington and I said to myself, "Hal, you're too tired to go. Why don't you hit the sack and get some studying done for your big tests on Tuesday?"

The other side of me responded, "But you promised! You must go. Something good is going to happen, even though you're very tired. Go ahead."

So I went. My friend Willie and I were driving along over those Kentucky hills. The blue grass was blowing in just the right direction. You could actually see the waves of blue sparkling under the afternoon sun. As we proceeded around another curve, we saw smoke and fire. Willie stopped the car and we dashed over to the left side of the road. A new black Cadillac was smashed into a tree. A man had been thrown out of the car. As we ran toward him the leaking gasoline burst into flames. Just in the nick of time we pulled the driver out and asked an approaching farmer to call for a rescue wagon. Within half an hour the man was strapped on to a stretcher and we lifted him into the ambulance. The driver asked me to stay beside the man while he drove him to the hospital. Riding along, completely in a state of shock, he started talking—"Who are you? What happened to me? Who am I? Where am I going?"

"Wow! What fantastic questions for a man to ask when he's completely in a state of shock!" I thought.

"You had an accident," I whispered in his ear. "We're taking you to a hospital. You're not alone," I said, but he didn't hear me.

We wheeled him into an emergency surgical room and waited to hear from the doctors. After an hour or two someone emerged and a man behind a green facial mask said, "Your friend may die. The top of his head was severely damaged, he has many broken bones, and he has a serious heart condition. I cannot give him even a fifty-fifty chance to live."

Every week I visited the hospital. My new friend was conscious during the first two or three visits. He was a very wealthy and unhappy man. He wasn't at all the churchy type, but he called me "preacher boy," and we'd talk and I'd rub his head or his hands and after a few minutes I'd say a prayer.

One day I came to visit him and his wife was standing in the hall. We spent a few minutes together. The nurse walked up and said, "Reverend, he's been unconscious for several days. He will not hear what you might have to say, but go ahead and spend a few minutes with him."

I felt a sense of gratitude for the nurse's sensitivity and I thanked her. The man was dying, and one could almost feel it throughout the room. I laid my hand on his forehead and rubbed him gently and prayed. "Father, thanks for giving me the opportunity to tell my brother about you. Help him feel loved and significant and forgiven and blessed right now. Speak directly to his unconscious, deeper than I could with human words, and enable him to surrender to your love . . . ."

Right in the middle of my prayer (I had my eyes open) he opened his eyes and started talking! "It's all right, Preacher Boy. I'm ready to go. It's all right."

I wasn't at all sure of what I thought I heard, but a glow of light around his face made me feel quite confident that God was doing something and everything *was* okay.

A week later I returned and, as usual, I checked in at the nurse's station before visiting a patient. "How's Mr. Brown doing today?" I asked.

The nurse opened a little book and quietly answered my question. "Mr. Brown passed away last week."

"Please," I said, "tell me exactly what time he died."

I wasn't surprised when she said he died just minutes after I left his room on my last visit. I felt very sober and close to God as I walked out to the parking lot. My new brother was with God. I was glad I made the decision I did on that particular Sunday or I would have missed this opportunity to celebrate God's love with my new friend.

One great thing that happened to me during those four years of college was the deep awareness and teaching I received about the indwelling Christ—the Holy Spirit. I shall never be able to express my gratitude to God for giving me a college like that at which to study and be a part of.

There is a double danger for those who attend so-called Christian colleges. There's the constant pressure to *perform* religiously, and there's the danger of being a culture-Christian without knowing what it means to experience the love of God for one's own sake or in a secular setting. My high school pastor was right—it would be helpful if I went to both settings—to a conservative college and then to a liberal seminary.

I did not agree with him for awhile during my college years. In fact, I identified with the very conservative and serious-minded Christians, and I played a religious game without knowing how phony and unchristian it was.

I'M GOING TO BE A CHRISTIAN IF IT KILLS ME

First of all, I became very narrow and legalistic. I wouldn't listen to the news on the radio because it was worldly. I stopped going to the movies and even felt my dad was going to hell if he didn't change jobs—and I let him know it with dozens of Scripture-packed letters! I was a very committed self-righteous and sometimes a loveless good guy!

Two-and-a-half beautiful years with my high school girlfriend were chopped into little pieces. I totally rejected them and labeled them satanic because we danced and did other "worldly" things together. I asked her to return my ring. I broke up with her because she wasn't religious enough and I did it *in the name of Jesus!*

I grew so religious and covered myself over with appropriately selected Scripture and doctrine. I found myself unable to cope emotionally. I used God to justify my prejudices, my choices, and my value system. I felt I was right because I was doing what I thought God wanted me to do. At least one thing was absent—knowledge about my inner feelings. Neither did I sense a conscious need for sharing at a depth level. In my theological and psychological studies I knew little or nothing about true community.

During certain moments of private introspection I did wonder why I had feelings of melancholy and depression. I was sure that more hours praying and studying the Scriptures would take these bad feelings away. I spent many many hours pouring through the Scriptures but those feelings persisted.

Nevertheless, beautiful things continued to happen. A dear man named Bill Webber walked up to me one day and paid my tuition for my entire senior year. My personal needs were met time and again in answer to prayers. It was undoubtedly an era of great faith and tremendous blessing from God, but something within was lost in the process. I admired and obeyed God to the best of my ability but I didn't love myself! My faith was okay, but my emotions were in a constant state of upheaval.

I often thought back to that moment of love at Lake Junaluska and the tremendous freedom I felt as a teenager when I first read through the Scriptures. I had lost that first love, and I didn't know how to get it back. I knew more *about* God, more *about* theology and psychology, and more *about* the Bible than ever, but I didn't love myself. The civil war inside was burning in my stomach. I didn't understand, and my only alternative was to keep on searching, keep on believing, keep on hoping for that gift of wholeness.

Jesus, as I see it, faith is your gift of receptivity in my life . . . and feelings are my emotional responses and reactions to that which is within and around me. My faith is how I relate to you and my feelings may or may not coincide with my commitment to you. Even though I may make a commitment from my will, I may still have lots of emotional blockades. Is that right? I think that's very true for me. I mean, is that a functional description of faith and feeling?

Sometimes I feel all sorts of things, sometimes I'm void of feeling. Sometimes I love you. Sometimes I hate you. You know it. Thank you for understanding me more than I'm capable of understanding myself.

Thank you for the miracle of relationship—and for the privilege of having . . . and working through . . . my feelings. My feelings. All of them. Thanks for faith, and for feelings.

7

Seminary

or

Cemetery?

1. Have you ever caught yourself sending non-verbal missiles to people—knowing all along that this was misplaced baggage? How can we help each other own our real feelings and express them in community?
2. Can you grow without hurting? It seems I can't. I don't like to admit that about myself. How do you experience your best growth?
3. What book or books were stabilizers in your Christian growth during your first years? Why did they help you? What specific insights or guidance did you get as a result of those books?

7

Seminary or Cemetery?

Mark 14:34—*Do you suppose Jesus experienced the pain you sometimes feel? Did he ever feel alone and in need of support?*
Mark 14:8—*How important is it to you to help the other person identify his or her gift.*
2 Corinthians 1:6–10—*Did you know that your new sensitivity and resources are related to the pain you've been through?*
Galatians 6:4–5—*Have you joined the human race yet?*

I feel a bit of inward pain as I begin communicating my feelings about seminary. I entered a well-known eastern seminary with naïve expectations. I honestly thought I had arranged the truth in a very biblical, therefore, highly acceptable, package. I also entered seminary with negative feelings about this particular theological school. My only goal was to get through seminary without losing my faith.

Seminary was a lonely and threatening experience. I enjoyed the weekends—when I served student pastorates some seventy-five miles away from the school—among those laymen in our little country churches. I rebelled and silently retreated within. At that time I couldn't admit to myself that I was unable to cope with (much less express) the feelings that emerged. I skipped chapel consistently. I slept through two classes regularly and made D's in those particular subjects. Rather than verbalize or admit my disagreement with a professor, I'd play Jonah's game and pull the shades down and sleep through the class. Because of my own theological prejudices I trusted myself only with those books, commentaries, and professors that had my conservative sounds. I was afraid to trust those "liberals." My defensive boxed-in bulldogmatic approach made me physically sick!

It actually came out my flesh! During that year in seminary my body absorbed the poison of my own painfully broken and repressed emotions. Because of this tremendous load of anxiety, I developed several sinus infections, allergies, throat problems, stomach tensions, and other problems, all of them directly affected by deeper emotional tension. This was the diagnosis of several doctors on the University Hospital staff.

To know that one's physical illness is intensified by emotional tension may give some people a sense of fulfillment, but I needed to know more than *why* I felt that way. I wanted to know *how* to change the situation. I tried to think through the last four years of pretheological training I received in college. I thought about my psychology courses. I wanted desperately to understand what I could do about the inner turmoil that was building up day after day.

During my seminary experience I did not find one person who knew how to help me with this inner tension. Day after day I pumped myself up to continue and get the degree and get out. I often wondered why I ever let myself get into the ministry. When I engaged in longer periods of introspection I questioned my vocation and with great struggling I'd voice my depression and frustration God-ward: "Lord, I think you've made a mistake—or I have. I'm feeling tremendously frustrated about my role in the church. I really don't know what it means to be a Christian minister. I thought I did. But I don't, and I need to express my doubt to you. If it weren't for the hope I still feel as a result of that experience I had with you, in that moment of love at Lake Junaluska, I believe I'd quit. Now, I'm totally exhausted, lonely, and completely incapacitated. I can't study. I don't seem to be communicating with the laymen in my churches. I'm not able to love myself. There's nothing I can hang on to . . . *but You.*"

Slowly new life would come, time and time again, when I prayed myself into a new surrender. The prayer-encounters came repeatedly and were quite healing once I really got in touch with those things down inside. Time and time again I experienced dark and seemingly endless emotional upheaval. This drove me to two things. First, I was made conscious of my human inadequacy. Second, I often stumbled into the reality of God's set of "higher facts." Dr. E. Stanley Jones often talked about two sets of facts. The lower key of facts focused on human need and perspective. He said we could push the shift button and surrender ourselves to a higher set of facts. Then we see through God's perspective and operate on a more redemptive and realistic level of life.

During one of those times of deep personal struggle and surrender I was greatly encouraged by something I read from one of the early church fathers. I can't find the source but I remember the quote: "Oh, the pain of knowing myself. Oh, the joy of knowing God!" It was helpful to know I wasn't alone.

One cold winter day I walked by an open window on my way to the library. I thought it rather odd that the window was open but I walked on past without shutting it. I didn't know until later that less than a minute before I walked by, one of my classmates jumped through that window to his death. I heard he spent several hours in private counseling with a professor and half a day praying in the chapel, after which he walked to the window from the chapel. For days I identified with that unknown classmate. In a way I knew him because I fantasized that it was I who had jumped. I admitted to myself some months later that I might very easily have jumped out of a window during that very rough year.

The seminary, you must understand, was not my problem. It was a symbol of what I experienced inside myself. I decided to stop my schooling. I did not have the emotional or physical energy to face another year. I did not go back the next year.

During that first year of seminary my wife, Betsy, and I lived in a rural community in eastern North Carolina and served three small churches. One of our three churches was located in the country. It was the oldest church in Green County. Our parsonage was an old farmhouse. An eighty-year-old lady owned the house. We shared half the house and used the same phone. Then we moved into an attic efficiency apartment. A huge billboard located on the property of one of our long-standing churchmen read, "Join the Ku Klux Klan! This is Klan Country!"

Our second church was located fifteen miles away in a new suburb. We received a pack of cards with prospective names and four acres of vacant property for a future church. For months we held little house churches. Through these small group sessions in the various living rooms of our community we developed beautiful personal relationships. You might say we had a small group church but Betsy and I, at this point in our ministry, knew absolutely nothing about small groups as a dynamic process.

Our third church was a very small group of unhappy people who really didn't want to start a new church, but at the insistence of our district superintendent they kept trying and I was appointed to help them get started.

During those early years of ministry I preached the love of God from the Scriptures, but I knew deep down inside that my inner tension was leaking out. I tried to avoid and dismiss it, but now and then I'd find myself saying certain words and using subtle illustrations which weren't what you would call healing or appropriate! Even though I never mentioned names, those nonverbal missiles always seemed to hit home. I don't recollect ever sharing angry feelings or frustrations with any of the members. Those unexpressed feelings would emerge and find their targets at the most inopportune times. I clothed my darts with the "Word of God." I made my point by quoting just the right Scripture to justify my values. I never did this with any conscious malice toward anyone. The subconscious and unconscious mind, I've learned, express themselves oftentimes without conscious self-knowledge. The real miracle, for me at least, was the way my laymen kept loving me anyway. Laymen helped me discover my humanity in more ways than one!

I enjoyed not going to seminary. I liked being with our churches full time. But I could not avoid finishing seminary if I wanted to be fully ordained in my denomination. A year later, after we moved to another pastorate, I returned to seminary by enrolling in one of another denomination. I was afraid I'd experience my former fears and behavior, but the opposite happened. Having grown up in one particular denomination all my life it was very refreshing to attend a seminary with new rituals, new sounds, different priorities, different attire. It was like viewing church history, liturgy, and theology from a different angle, and it was great! Participating in the Eucharist, singing Gregorian chants, being free to come and go without political connections—all this motivated me and gave me encouragement. I graduated from seminary on October 31st and the Old Testament lesson for that day was my favorite Psalm: Psalm 130. "Out of the depths of despair I cry for your help. Hear me! Answer! Help me!"

He did!

I'm glad I listened to Jack's advice. He knew I had to work through my own pain in order to comprehend something of where the church is today. Had I limited myself to only one theological stance, I'm sure my lifestyle and ministry would have a totally different value system.

Dr. E. Stanley Jones' devotional books *(The Way, The Word Become Flesh)* were stabilizers in my theological search during those five years. In one of these devotional books I read, "It takes all the sons of men to begin to say what the Son of man has said."

I thought about the wide variety of people who came into my life.

In college I listened to men who presented the conservative biblical view of the church and Christian growth. They talked about the priorities of conversion, prayer, Scripture reading, growth (or the process called sanctification), and evangelistic proclamation. During my first year of seminary I heard men talk about priorities involving social concern, analysis of the biblical text, the necessity of corporate community, and the importance of intellectual discipline. Tremendous emphasis was placed on how to lead a worship service, what to wear, how to perform. An intellectual grasp of the ancient languages was imperative.

I'm glad seminary happened to me. Going through theological school with my set of needs and values taught me something about the pain and joy many of you experience as you go through initial years of vocational preparation. Now I know what some of you feel when you go through similar struggles. At that time I thought my pain was unique. Stretching and incorporating new ideas and grasping facts wasn't easy for me. I'm glad it wasn't. It still isn't easy!

I BURIED WHAT I DIDN'T WANT TO BE

Seminary was a kind of cemetery for me. I died many times during those years. And I was brought alive by God in the process.

It was a cameo of life—a time to suffer, to die, to be born again. If that's what seminaries are for, then they succeeded in my personal growth.

Thanks for helping me die . . . time and time again. I guess we all have our own cemeteries, and no one likes to die. At least, I don't . . . .

I've thought about my fellow classmate who jumped out the window to his death. That's one way to die. I'm glad there are other ways to die in order to deal with the painful things that exist within and around me.

Thank you, Jesus, for a safe place to die—a place where you take over the situation and me. Thank you for bringing me back into the land of the living, and for the ability to enjoy life without a trace of guilt!

8

Guess Who You Married?

1. What specific gifts do you celebrate most in your spouse? How does he/she show love and respect to you? What do you do that expresses love and respect for him/her?
2. What demands, or impediments, keep you and your spouse from communicating more creatively? Are you expecting him/her to change first? How do you feel when you ask yourself this question?
3. Have you found someone who listens to you both and helps you both feel, and fight, your way to new feelings of self-worth in your marriage? How do you find those people who can hear and enable you both along?
4. What extra baggage did you bring into your marriage—baggage that needs unloading? When was the last time you said "I am wrong?" What are you going to do about this extra baggage without hiding it or violating anyone? What alternatives do you have?

8

Guess Who You Married?

Ephesians 5:25, 28, 33—*How can husbands and wives and their children do each other a real favor?*
1 Peter 3:1-3—*What can a wife do that really speaks to her husband?*
1 Peter 4:10—*Did you know that your marriage possesses special abilities and potential for greatness?*
James 5:16—*What happens if/when you admit your humanity to each other in the context of Christian community?*

"She's a gal I'd like to date sometime," I thought as I day-dreamed during science class.

I first met Betsy during our freshman year in college. We ran against each other for vice-president of the freshman class. For two years we did not date. Whenever I had problems with my dates, I'd talk to Bets. She was a good listener, and we enjoyed a casual friendship. Both of us were going steady with someone else.

During Christmas vacation of our junior year my girlfriend and I broke up and, incidentally, Betsy and her boyfriend broke up, too. When I returned from vacation and learned that Betsy was available I asked her for a date. Because she and my girlfriend were such close friends they had to work things out between themselves before she'd consent to go out with me!

The following year was filled with the wonderful wine of courtship. We spent hours and hours talking, dreaming, sharing personal feelings. We both retraced our entire past as much as possible, and we thought of our relationship as a very special gift to both of us. We decided to get married. Whenever we went out on special occasions, like a banquet or artist series, I ordered six red roses to celebrate our time together. The red rose became a symbol of our relationship. We decided that a rose emerged into the fullness of its own uniqueness without anybody touching it. Indeed, we realized that if we forced the petals, we'd bruise them. The message of the rose has been a constant reminder to each of us—to honor each person's own ability to open up at his or her own pace.

The week leading up to our wedding was hilariously hectic with final exams and graduation rehearsals. We packed all our belongings, carefully placing everything into two distinct piles. One pile was to go to Florida with us on our honeymoon; the other was to go to North Carolina in my parents' car. We stayed up until 4:00 A.M. the morning before making arrangements so we would have a smooth wedding day.

Every day we checked the post office and opened letters from relatives and friends. Many envelopes contained notes of congratulations and money. By the end of the week we had received over $200. Almost all these letters and gifts came from people we seldom or ever communicated with. One of these letters came from the Reverend John Lewis, a dear old minister who devoted his entire life to the poor people in the Kentucky mountains. He traveled to all the churches and picked up furniture and clothes to distribute among the poverty-stricken families. I wept when I unfolded a ten dollar bill. His note read, "Hal and Betsy, this comes to you with God's love and blessing on your marriage. While I was praying this morning, the Lord led me to send this to you."

My roommate and a few other fellows in our dorm came into my room with a surprise. "Hal, all the guys in our dorm wanted to do a little something for you and Betsy. We took up a collection to pay for the flowers and the rental of the chapel. You give us the bills and we'll take care of those expenses as our gift to you both."

The big day finally arrived. We graduated in the morning and were married that afternoon. Many of our college friends attended the wedding. Moments before time to walk out into the sanctuary I grew so weak and frightened I had to sit down on the floor. The Wedding March sounded, my friends helped me to my feet, and fourteen minutes later we were married "in the name of the Father, the Son and the Holy Spirit."

Our green Rambler station wagon was packed to the hilt. We drove away with friends and relatives waving their hands and laughing at tin cans bouncing behind, paper banners flapping from the radio aerial, and lipstick messages all over the car. Our eyes sparkled with excitement. We thought marriage was going to be something special. We figured that we'd shared so much during the past year that *this* marriage of *ours* wouldn't have the problems other people had. After all, we believed God wanted us to be together, and we were very open and honest. Besides, we prayed together. Little did we know.

DID WE BRING EVERYTHING WE NEED?

The little green bug headed south through the blue grass toward Florida. Three hundred miles later our marriage encountered it's first jolt. I opened the back door to get Betsy's suitcases and I couldn't believe my eyes! The back was full of books, dishes and other stuff you just don't take on a honeymoon. We were carrying what seemed to be a ton of useless cargo. There had been a big mistake! We were stuck with a load of stuff that was meant for my parents' car! That incident became a monumental parable. We brought a *lot* of hidden cargo into our marital relationship! This was only the first of many surprises in store for us.

I am the oldest of four boys and out of sheer ignorance I naturally assumed that girls were built with similar emotional responses. All four of us were highly competitive. We wrestled our way through childhood together, so of course, I assumed that my wife would be the same type.

While on our honeymoon I found a dead water snake. I decided to take it to the motel. As I walked back with the harmless little creature dangling from my hand, I thought about the times my brothers and friends teased me with snakes, turtles, and other small creatures. We had fun teasing each other. I figured she'd slap the snake out of my hand and throw it back at me and we'd run after each other. Then, my fantasy continued, we'd wrestle and hug and kiss and laugh over the whole game. I took the snake into the room and woke up to reality the hard way. That snake scared the daylights out of her. I was taken back in total dismay! She didn't play the game! I was mortally wounded when she expressed such intense anger as I had never experienced with her during our four years of knowing each other in college. Besides, she locked me out for the rest of the day.

I thought our marriage would be different because we were Christians; I'd seen other marriages, and we were both very determined that ours would be so much better. The idealistic sparkle of youth demanded better things. Even after the snake incident, I never dreamed that we were just beginning to experience more tension and misunderstanding.

We began our marriage in the midst of my seminary training. The undercurrent of tension and anxiety mounted. We tried to communicate, but there were too many adjustments, too many *other* demands. We had no one we could turn to regarding our personal relationships. We knew no one whom we trusted with our subtle marital walls.

We stopped trying to reach out; however, we didn't stop praying for God's guidance. Before we were married we decided never to go to bed without working through our anger. Often we talked until two or three o'clock in the morning, sometimes two or three days a week. We were wearing ourselves out. We did what many couples do . . . we kept struggling and experimenting. But the wall continued to grow between us. Whenever we came too close to pain we avoided it and each other. Somehow, we both knew what not to talk about. So we quietly avoided the obvious points of tension! Often we sat in horrible silence because we could not approach each other realistically and honestly without encountering too much pain. Finally, one bleak morning Betsy said, "Hal, we simply can't live this way any longer. Our communications have to change or we can't live together. Something is going to break."

I nodded silently. I was afraid to say, "Yes, I've felt this for sometime, but I wouldn't admit it."

We both knew and finally verbalized the fact that a deep chasm was between us and we couldn't have a real marriage without making a change. We were not disloyal to each other. We had what you might call a very good marriage. We prayed together daily. We spent many hours helping other people every day. We were doing many good things. We traveled about and enjoyed a lot of things. We saw some positive growth in our churches. But we were coming to a point of relational desperation. Depleted emotionally, we consciously prayed together for a new depth of wholeness—wholeness we knew nothing about. We hoped for better days.

WHERE ARE WE?

We had no idea that God was using this tension to help move us toward wholeness. Neither of us understood our discomfort and pain as a means of moving us toward the object of our prayers. At that time I wondered why we ever got married. I thought about what a psychologist told me, "Hal, this marriage will not work."

God did answer our prayers. He gave us the opportunity to meet new people and find a community of caring communicators. We moved to an inner city church where I served as youth pastor and finally finished my last two years of seminary. The senior pastor of this local church led Betsy and me into new discoveries. Phil enabled us to listen and understand. He helped us feel new feelings, ones of affirmation and self-worth. He engaged us in helping each other see some new answers within ourselves. Significant changes came during the four years we lived in that city. We could measure these changes, even though it came slowly and painfully.

Years passed. Our family kept growing. I became absorbed in my vocation. We moved to the West Coast. I spent more and more time with my work and less quality time with my wife and children.

Betsy kept busy living out the pastor's wife syndrome and I played the role of the very active and always available benevolent pastor who extended his good nature at all times—day and night. Actually, I extended myself out of my family. No evenings at home, fewer fun times, no time to disengage or pick daisies. Even the times we had together as a family were often rushed. Our lives were so full with meetings and people, we didn't know how to unwind even when we did have a few days away. I experienced tremendous guilt (which I couldn't even admit to myself, by the way) whenever I wasn't working on a sermon, or visiting a sick patient, or getting to know a new prospective member, or attending a key committee. I was a workaholic and didn't know it.

I enjoyed my day off only when I went away from home. When our children were pre-school age we'd go to the beach every Monday. Those were precious days of relaxation, fun, and creative quietness for all of us. I had to remove myself geographically from my home in order to relax. When I puttered about the house on my "day off" the phone would ring and another important mission was on the way. What got me most were those people who just "happened" to show up when I messed around in my garage workbench. Inevitably someone would say, "Gee, I wish my husband could get time off in the middle of the week like you. It must be great being a preacher and having time to do things like that around the house. My husband

. . . bla . . . bla . . . bla," they'd say. My own battles over personal acceptance and responsibility rang all kinds of bells down inside of me and I would clog up with enough false guilt to ruin the rest of my "day off."

I was one of those people who seldom relaxed in childhood. Somehow I had the idea that "doing nothing" was a waste of time. Did you ever hear that "Idle hands are the Devil's workshop"? I carried this over into my adult behavior. It's been only a few years now since I've been honest enough to admit even to myself that I've made a god out of my vocation. I used my commitment of time and energy in my vocation as one way to assure myself that "I am committed to God, and I am doing a good job."

But "doing a good job" as a clergyman can drain all the life and energy one possesses if he goes about it as a *means* of making himself whole.

My vocation was tied in very closely to my own identity struggle. Once I started dealing with deeper areas of my identity, making myself openly accountable to a few loving and honest people, I became more aware of these hidden parts of my daily lifestyle.

This neurotic pace did something to our marriage. I was out "having all the fun" with lots of different people and I left my wife home with dishes, dusters, and diapers. We often talked about how important it is to have one day off each week, to *be* together, and to have an occasional evening out alone—just the two of us. We even put it on our calendar, but we (rather I) often let it slip because "something important" would come up.

Both of us felt the need to be involved in a therapy group led by a woman who had what we called "the gift of negative caring." She had the ability to smell out a rat and call it by name and it was not easy to work on these new areas! Betsy attended a group including mostly pastor's wives, and I attended my group every Thursday from noon until two o'clock with nine other clergymen. We attended this group for more than a year. The therapist didn't profess to be a Christian, but God really used her in my own life! Through this secular friend, and others along the way, I've become utterly convinced that God does a lot of healing for many of us "Christian" types. Through these experiences I've learned (with tremendous relief) that God is much bigger than we who claim to be Christians!

During that year of group involvement Betsy and I became more aware of our marital games. For many years Betsy would not deal with her true feelings about the way I was relating to our family. And, I admit, I had a lot of anxiety and repressed hatred for her. I've often operated out of guilt and couldn't, or wouldn't, dare admit this to myself.

I poured myself into many personal relationships day after day. I spent many hours listening and sharing with individuals and groups. I would come home emotionally exhausted and drained clear down to my toes. The last thing I wanted to do, and the first thing I needed to do, was to listen to my wife and kids! Betsy felt this and she often kept her feelings down because she wanted me to relax. Besides, she learned how awful it was to get one more put-down from me when I'd act like I was listening, but we both knew I was really not there. To *act like* a listener and to *be* an active listener are two different things.

A crisis emerged during Christmas. Between the two of us we had invited over sixty people into our home for a series of full-course dinners. I came home and announced, "Honey, you remember so-and-so? Well, we had a great time talking and I just felt *we* (notice the all-inclusive and controlling *we*) needed to include him on Friday night when we have the Jones' family over. Is that okay?"

Wham! All hell broke loose. "Hal Edwards," she screamed. Immediately I knew something new was about to explode with tremendous intensity. "You and your damn church can go to hell! I've had enough. I simply can't take it any more!"

I couldn't believe my eyes or ears. My wife, a preacher's wife, the daughter of a pastor, and the granddaughter of a pastor, screaming at the top of her voice. At first I wondered if the neighbors heard her screaming. Then I felt ashamed that I cared what others thought. Then I came in touch with my own real feelings and I knew she was right. She was so real, and I knew in a flash that our whole future was hanging in the balance. Betsy was saying out loud what I was afraid to say. I lay on the bed beside her and after quite awhile I decided to talk. "Honey, I need help, too. I've hidden this stuff inside long enough. Thanks for having the guts to say it. I hope I can be honest enough and open enough to change."

For days after that episode I found myself reviewing my behavior and my values. For once I didn't run away from my pain and I was finally able to see myself in a new perspective. I immediately shared this with two or three close friends in our church and, to my surprise, I discovered they had known about this all along! What a supernatural gift—to have a few lovers in one's own church, lay persons who really care! These people helped me become accountable to my wife and children in the midst of these new personal insights. Without their constant encouragement and honesty I do not know what my personal growth would have been.

Something started clicking in our marriage. A new depth of understanding emerged over the next six months as a result of this experience. I felt a new appreciation for Betsy and her ability to say what she felt. We had played "preacher and wife" so long that we found it terribly awkward to deal with negative feelings. With the

NOW WE'RE READY TO TAKE A NEW LOOK AT THINGS

help of the group, and through a new awareness of a deeper meaning of Christian love, we came into a new appreciation for both negative *and* positive love. When we do trust each other with negative (as well as some risky positive) feelings, we know that something real is happening between us. Our marriage, therefore, our ministry, developed a new quality because we were consciously commiting ourselves to grow towards healthier communications.

We still find it hard to share deep feelings from time to time. A dream, a fantasy, a feeling of lust for the opposite sex or each other —these are constant symbols of my humanity. I think I'm always going to be faced with the risk of dealing with my real feelings and growing creatively.

I don't think any one couple can be the model for others to follow. What seems right and workable for Betsy and myself, or in your marriage, may not work at all in someone else's. Someone else's style of sharing may not fit our marriage. However, we can "own" our true feelings and encourage each other to take new risks toward wholeness. We are both excited about the possibility of constant growth and maturity, even though it never comes easy. At least, we haven't found it easy, nor do we expect our marriage to be easy in the future.

In closing this chapter I must tell you about today. I've been baby-sitting all day. Betsy is late for supper and I spent all afternoon making a beautiful supper to surprise her. Everything was timed perfectly —except for one thing—Betsy hasn't shown up. I felt let down, and then I recalled all the many evenings when I didn't get home on time because I was doing "the Lord's work." It sure makes a difference when I find myself on the other side of the picture!

Lord, years after the day we both said "I do" I can even thank you for the extra baggage we took on our honeymoon! I'll never forget that carload of junk.

Thank you for helping married couples (like Betsy and me) sort out the meaning of the junk we bring into our marriages.

Some of that junk has become valuable treasure because we were forced to deal with the hidden meanings behind it all. The job isn't finished by any means, but it feels great to know that we are committed to you, to life, and to each other.

Marriage sure isn't easy, Lord. But it is tremendously rewarding to stick with the creative commitments and options you've lined up for us.

9

Hey, Dad,
Where
'Ya Going Now?

1. What are your children trying to say to you about your relationship to them *this week?* What does their behavior mirror? How do you evaluate your relationships with each child? Are you ready to do something about the broken relationships? If so, what?
2. How would you describe the particular gifts of each of your children? What are these children teaching you about the amount and the quality of time you spend together?
3. Is your identity so tied into your vocation that you cannot earn your right to be respected as a friend or parent? What are your feelings about this?
4. Have you become a child with a child in the last two months? What happened to the child inside you?

9

Hey, Dad, Where 'Ya Going Now?

Ephesians 6:4—*What do children do when we put them down?*
1 Peter 3:8-10—*What does a healthy family model look like?*
Mark 10:15—*How can you become a little child and enjoy God's presence in simplicity?*
Luke 15:20—*When did you ever see your father run and embrace you and welcome you when you didn't deserve it? What does this story tell you about your relationship with your parents/children?*

Children have a way of teaching their parents a great many things —whether or not parents want to learn! Somehow, children have a way of sneaking up on their parents without anyone knowing it. I've often wondered if I haven't overlooked one of the greatest resources in the world when I neglect to consider my own children as among my most effective teachers.

Of course, parents teach children and can't escape being significant models of learning for them. We register in their lives what we do and what we do not do. How we feel, what we value, what we like to do, how we eat and sleep, how we judge certain people—all these things make tremendous impacts upon our children, no matter what age they are.

In this chapter, however, I'd like to turn it all around, and share some things my children have taught me. They don't know this, I'm sure. And your children have no idea they're teaching you, either. But they do teach us valuable lessons about ourselves—if we let them.

For a long long time I didn't give my children the opportunity to teach me a thing. I thought it was my responsibility, rather our responsibility as parents, to do *all* the teaching. Things happened. Our children started walking and talking. The house was constantly full of interruptions. "I want this. I want to go, too. Why don't you give some to me, too? What about me?"

New questions, new priorities, new everything—*always.* With four children things shift so fast we hardly have time to be bored.

When Sam was about three years old he loved purple and anything with wheels captured his imagination. So, he constantly played with little purple cars. One night I was hurrying about in my bedroom dressing for another church meeting. He was talking purple wheel language and I played as though I were listening, but I had my mind on the meeting. Right in the middle of my daydreaming I was sharply criticized. "Hey, Dad, you aren't *listening* to me!" he screamed out.

"Sure I am, son," I automatically responded. But I knew he was right. I went on to the meeting but his little voice resounded over and over again, "You aren't listening to me. . . . You aren't listening to me."

Three or four days later I was hurrying out for another meeting. It was a beautiful evening and I decided to walk. The summer sunset was glorious. The palm trees swayed in the gentle breeze. I was half a block from the house when I heard that same little boy's shrill voice. I knew immediately it was Sam. "Hey, Daaaaaad! Where 'ya goin' NOW?"

I continued walking without responding. All the way to church I thought about my boy's little voice and the message that spoke the big truth! Do I say, "Son, I'm leaving you every night like this so I can tell other people how they can love Jesus and their families" or do I say, "Son, you'll understand when you get to be a parent"?

The trustee meeting was a waste of time and more guilt emerged as I sat there. While these men complained about the way the junior high school kids across the street were ruining church property, I wanted to cry or run or do something wild. But I just sat there and kept quiet and played my game. When I returned home after the meeting everyone was in bed except Betsy. I didn't tell her about the meeting but I did tell her that something was happening inside me and Sam's little voice triggered it with his question, "Where 'ya going now?"

I was deeply moved as Betsy and I shared late that night. I felt God was teaching me a crucial lesson. He was speaking to me through the voice of a little child because I was putting church work ahead of my own family. I could understand why my children didn't respect me. I finally understood why they resented me. I was not living close enough to earn my right to be respected. As a result of that experience, I made some definite changes in our family schedule.

Libby, our oldest daughter, taught me a tremendous lesson about forgiveness and honesty. It so happened that the choir director affirmed my voice and asked me to sing a solo on a certain Sunday. I was so flattered I said yes. I went home and searched for an old favorite of mine, The 130th Psalm. I sang that solo in a music festival ages ago during high school. Betsy helped me as I practiced the song. During the practice session, Libby walked into the living room. She stopped dead still and then fell into hilarious laughter. "Dad, what on earth are you doing?"

Hot resentment rose up from my feet to my head! I was so angry I reached over and slapped her. Then, with controlled reverence I answered, "I'm *practicing* for Sunday, what do you think I'm doing!"

I WAS SWINGING AT MYSELF AND HITTING OTHERS

Betsy sat stunned on the piano bench. Libby, totally taken back with the unexpected wallop from her father, sobbed and ran to her room. There I stood like the jackass I was. I didn't even look at Betsy. I walked toward Libby's bedroom, opened the door and sat down beside the bed. She was pouring it on as kids do when they have their parents over a barrel. But I kept quiet for a long time and then I spoke up. "Libby, maybe you don't need to hear this, but I guess I need to say it. I was wrong. I've always asked you to be honest with me, and this time you were—and I punished you for it. I know why I slapped you. It wasn't because you laughed at me. It was because I was mad at myself."

She sat up and wiped the tears away and continued listening. "You see, honey, I really don't want to sing. I said I'd sing a song in church next Sunday, but I'm angry because I lied to myself. So, I swung at myself and hit you. Please forgive me. I'm all uptight because I'm a phony. I'm not being honest with myself."

There was a little silence and then Libby jumped out of bed into my lap and kissed me and said, "Daddy, I do forgive you."

What a gift she gave me. She released me. She set her dad free from a great deal of inward pain. I shared this experience with the congregation before I sang the song. Incidentally, I changed the song to one which illustrated what had happened to me that day. I sang, "You'll Never Walk Alone," because I didn't feel alone. I felt loved and forgiven.

Our children usually respond to physical affection. That wasn't always the case with Joanna. She didn't respond the way I expected when I'd say, "How about a kiss?" or, "Come and sit with Dad. I'll rock you." That threatened me at first; because all the other kids took to kissing and hugging and rocking like fish to water. Instead, she'd just look at me and walk on as though I hadn't said a word. My first impulse was to force her to "respect her parents" and make her respond. Instinctively I began to recognize my own need to dominate her freedom. So, I relaxed and dropped it. Then when I least expected it, Joanna flew into my arms of her own accord and hugged and kissed me and then walked away.

Last week she brought in a bouquet of wild flowers and danced through the room. I thought about my childhood and the time I felt guilty because I didn't want to show affection to a "favorite" aunt. I faked it. Joanna's teaching me not to fake it. Her kisses weren't for sale, and even her dad couldn't violate her love.

One night as we were sitting together at supper, Rachel and Sam

WHAT'S INSIDE ME?

had an argument. When I called Rachel down, she threw her fork on the table, burst into tears, and ran to her bedroom, slammed the door and locked it. I decided to let her stay alone. Fifteen minutes passed. Supper was over and I was in the kitchen with Betsy when one of the children came down. "Dad, you'd better go talk with Rachel."

When I walked into her room I immediately noticed a three-inch hole in the wall, and Rachel was sobbing quite deeply. Betsy had just finished wall-papering the room. "What's happening inside, Rachel? Listen, Sweetheart, I know that Sam isn't your real problem. It's something else. If you want to talk to me I promise I'll simply be quiet and be your friend and stay with you."

"I can't stand it! I can't take it anymore," she screamed through her tears. "I don't like the way I'm acting with my friend. I don't know how to tell her what I want to do, and I'm all swallowed up. I can't turn off, and I feel awful inside."

I knew then what made the hole in the wall. It was Rachel's wrestling with what she thought she had to do to feel accepted by her special friend. We talked for about an hour and she finally worked it through. I told her how I admired her because I didn't know how to express my hurts when I was her age. I really did admire her, and we laughed about the "holy" hole. We decided to bury some things in that hole, mainly her feeling that she had to be responsible for her friends. The next day she went to school and worked it out with her teacher and her friend. I was so proud of her!

It's often so easy to miss the meaning behind our children's violent moments. I'm often blocked because I automatically react without giving the child time to communicate what's going on inside. I'm also confident that there are times when parents need to deal quickly with certain situations. I'm so glad I listened to Rachel. She taught me how important it is to process those violent emotions swirling about inside. I'll never forget that night. We felt so close and so inwardly cleansed, and we thanked God for the hole in the wall!

I'm asking God to show me how to enjoy the "child" inside of me. I don't think this necessarily means giving my adulthood away. Our children often involve me in their play. Play is the sacred work of children and because of them I'm learning to play again. They help me disengage and relax. They are showing me how play is a dynamic of God's grace. I really enjoy letting my own "child" out, because there are times when I feel like a child.

Here are some things we've found that matter a lot to our children: signs of affirmation, allowances, sharing school papers, playing games after supper, riding bikes together, rubbing backs during prayer time, saying "thank you" and "I'm sorry," and family vacation time. Perhaps the best way we parents can encourage our children is to give them some listening time, certainly in the midst of a crisis, but also during simple quiet walks around the block or to the nearest playground. I think we need to encourage our children to ask for this whenever they feel a need for it.

Most of us are aware of the imperfections of our parenthood! The verse of Scripture, "Unless you become as a little child, you shall not enter the kingdom of God" (Mark 10:15), is such an exciting word! Our children can teach us how to be open and have fun and not take life so seriously. When I forget this, I make myself into a vocational or sociological robot who plays emotional and spiritual games. God is so good! He gives us children so we can know how to be a child again—a child of God who celebrates the simple gifts of life. It's my belief that it's never too late to start. Nothing's really ever lost once we experience grace. We can pick up with each other at any given point because of God's fantastic grace!

Jesus refused to push the children away. I've noticed that when I am free to be myself, I don't find children so much trouble!

Jesus, thanks for teaching me how to play again. For so long I thought that being an adult meant that I couldn't play anymore. There's a beautiful little child in me and he still enjoys letting it all hang out. He still wants to have fun, be held, and enjoy the simple things of life.

Thanks for children who call the child out of me. Thanks for games and fireplaces and footballs and stuffed animals and all the things that help me share with children.

How wise you are to illustrate greatness by focusing on a child nearby. I want to experience greatness in my inward child—the kind of greatness that you made me to enjoy.

Jesus, I accept your gift to me—the gift of being a blessed child. A child of God.

10

My Parson's Mask
Is Stuck!

1. What three feeling-descriptions best describe how you feel about your vocation? What do you do that makes you feel self-worth? Do you find yourself so busy *doing* that you neglect *being* yourself?
2. Some people are more in control when they *give*. Some feel more comfortable *receiving*. How do you feel most comfortable or controlling, when you give or receive? Why?
3. Tell somebody about a relationship that has freed you from vocational paralysis. Who helped you know that you are not your vocation? How did that person free you up?
4. What happened to you that gave you the strength to ask the risky questions concerning your own vocational fulfillment? What happened? What did you do about it?

10

My Parson's Mask Is Stuck!

Galatians 5:13—*Do you have the freedom to love and serve others?*
Ephesians 3:20—*What's your expectancy-level with God regarding your ability to produce?*
Philippians 2:13—*Do you want to learn how to obey?*
Acts 9:17—*How does God send us to do specific things for others?*

In the front cover of my first *Book of Discipline* are written these words, dated December, 1952: "Hal, may the richest blessings of God be upon you in your efforts as you begin service in the greatest fellowship in all the world—The Methodist Church. Keep submissive to the Lord's will and work always toward the salvation of lost men."

This book was given me by my pastor when I received my local preacher's license. At seventeen years of age I knew what I wanted for the rest of my life. I wanted to be a preacher! Becoming a fully ordained clergyman in The Methodist Church meant four years of college and three years of seminary, but finally, the day came when I was ordained.

Grateful and elated, I knelt before the annual conference while the bishop and district superintendents laid hands upon my head and read these words: "The Lord pour upon thee the Holy Spirit for the office and work of an elder in the Church of God, now committed unto thee by the authority of the church through the imposition of our hands. And be thou a faithful dispenser of the Word of God, and of his holy Sacraments; in the name of the Father, and of the Son, and of the Holy Spirit. Amen."

SO THIS IS THE WAY THE CHURCH WORKS

Everyone congratulated us. Laymen and clergymen stood in line to welcome us into the fellowship and full membership of the conference. I was relieved and felt quite excited about my new ecclesiastical credentials. "Now, I'm *really* an equipped clergyman," I thought to myself. However, a gnawing fear began growing inside. "What if I fail? What if I can't live up to those beautiful words of ordination? Am I sure I know what it means to be a fully equipped clergyman? Why don't I feel more complete within?"

I asked Betsy to take a long quiet walk with me after the ordination service that night. We walked for an hour or two in total silence. As a result of finally receiving my ordination, I felt an emotional impact that opened up a flood of memories. For several years prior to my ordination I had been under close examination by a Ministerial Board of Qualifications Committee. One of the questions asked by this committee was, "Do you promise to abstain totally from the use of tobacco or any alcoholic beverages?" Four of the men on that particular committee smoked constantly. I was asked to write a 2,000 word paper on, "What I Believe," and I learned from the Board's responses and reactions to my paper that it served as a whipping post for those who judged others whose theological stance was quite dif-

ferent. Over those years I built up a lot of personal hostility for
Ministerial Qualification Committees. I felt abused and manipulated
by some of the men serving on this particular committee.

A few years ago in a clergy-and-wives sharing group I expressed
my feelings about these experiences to a friend in the group. "I have
a feeling, and I hope you will stay with me, because it involves you.
You remind me of a man who once served as Chairman of a Ministerial Board of Qualifications Committee. He frightened me and I felt
abused by him. I really hated that guy's guts. I don't know why, but
I feel the freedom to share this with you."

Ed's face became red and his wife laughed. A few others laughed
and I didn't understand until he explained to me that he was currently serving in that same position in his local conference! That encounter brought relief and sheer joy to us all!

I knew that preaching the Gospel—proclaiming the Good News
about the life and death and resurrection of Jesus Christ—was the
most important mission in the world. This was to be my fulltime
occupation. It was not to be taken lightly. I felt caught in a paradox,
and I didn't know how to deal with it. Preaching the Good News was
indeed the greatest calling. However, I felt like a hypocrite because
the wholeness I talked about in the pulpit was way beyond me. I
couldn't model that kind of perfection! I did not leave room for my
own humanity. I did not know how to share and celebrate my humanity in Christ. It seemed impossible to trust my lay people with
what I really felt and how I actually behaved.

How hard it was to think about sharing emotions experienced at a
deeper level. I was afraid that if I were to open up it would be too
much for anyone. After all, I thought, they looked up to me to be
their minister. It was my duty to try to serve them with every ounce
of courage, strength, and energy in my body and mind. It was my
privilege and duty to perform the work of the ministry—and to do
that meant sacrificing what I really wanted for myself. I poured myself into the work of the ministry. I wanted to be responsible and
obedient, never realizing that even this was in fact a denial of grace
and quite unbiblical in reality.

I had no idea at that time that I was negating the grace of Jesus
in me. That's strong language, but because I was locked up inside
myself I didn't trust God or people with my ministry much of the
time. I covered up my real feelings by going to meetings.

I thought I was creating a healthy atmosphere and modeling commitment. The truth is, I became so busy and so much in control that I undermined my lay people and their ability to minister. It was frightfully hard to trust God with his laity.

IT'S ME!

I was totally committed. At least, I was as committed as I knew how to be. I was so "committed" that I didn't know how to relax. Everywhere I went I wanted God to use me. I thought of my ministry as a twenty-four-hour lifestyle. I was stuck with a mask—a ministerial mask. My ministerial mask even smiled when I was crying. It would show up at meetings with an expression of adequacy and availability when I really felt very inadequate, pushed, tired, and lonely. My mask kept performing week after week, month after month, year after year. I wore it so long my face was forgotten. The mask became my face. I had become my vocation.

Something was happening inside of me. I came across, even to my wife and children, as a professional listener and counselor. I didn't let them know me as a person. I was so very busy giving, that it never crossed my mind that I had lost the art of receiving.

"Why don't you smile anymore?" a friend asked me over lunch one day. I must have depressed him with my serious messianic glance. I couldn't admit my hurt and loneliness to anyone at that time; I immediately avoided my true feelings and conversed about something else, something "spiritual." I usually avoided the deeper question and manipulated the conversation so that I might "help" the other person.

That kind of game playing sometimes led me to seriously question my own identity and the validity of my vocation. I knew something was wrong but I didn't know what. This glass wall between myself, my family and the people in our church remained intact.

One day I asked myself in the mirror, "My friend, what is the role of the clergy? Why are you caught in this stupid little syndrome? What do you want to do about it? What does it mean to communicate wholeness?"

The answers to those questions did not come immediately, but they did come gradually over a period of years. I met a man. I read a book. I began noticing a surprising awareness of growth taking place during small group experiences.

I'VE FOUND THE CHURCH AGAIN

One man who made a difference was a clergyman. He was the kind of person you immediately feel at home with. He, Betsy, and I sat together for fifteen minutes in the middle of a noisy downtown hotel lobby. People were coming and going but the three of us were wonderfully engaged in a very timely and creative conversation. Something unlocked inside! The experience of God's love in that threesome took me back to the time I was seventeen at Lake Junaluska. Here I was in a hotel lobby, exactly ten years later, experiencing that same depth of love. The man gave us no answers. It was the simple, open way in which he listened. That's right, it was the quiet unassuming delicate quality of his listening that gave God the room to move in closer. I'm sure my friend wasn't aware of the impact of our encounter. He was simply being himself. I can't remember anything profound he said; in fact, I can't remember *anything* he said. But I do remember being in the midst of a most creative relationship. Betsy and I walked out of the hotel and she knew something was bursting open inside of me. "Honey, I've found the church again! I know what to look for now. I see where my priorities are. This is what we've been looking for."

She nodded with tears in her eyes. We felt alive again and held hands on our way to the parking lot.

I suppose that being a clergyman I struggle with my faith—or the lack of it—as much as the next person. God seems very far away at times. Then there are days when I think I could reach out and touch him in person.

The greatest thing about the Christian ministry is the daily opportunity to enrich my own life with the lives of others. Being in the ministry means dealing with lots of people—from the pulpit, in smaller gatherings, in times of joy or heartbreak. It means going with people on their journey, enabling them to develop and reproduce a resourceful Christian lifestyle.

Helping others experience the power of love is very rewarding; however, I must constantly make myself accountable to a few others so that I will grow and receive. I think it's imperative to make ministry a mutual exchange. I've learned it's not enough to help other people, it is necessary sometimes to seek help from the very people I'm trying to help. That's why I have attended therapy groups and belong to a small group. Mutual sharing helps prevent me from getting locked into a narrow messianic self-image. Besides, where I am weak, my brother or sister will often help me by hearing my silent scream or by clearing up my misplaced sense of priority.

Being a clergyman *alone* has been my most painful kind of lone-liness. How horrible it is to feel cut off, aloof, naïve, and unrelatable. I've wept many tears (alone) in the church study. I can remember several times when I beat my fists into the floor and begged God to take the pressure off and release me. I recall moments of sheer fright and utter insecurity before worship services. Time and time again these experiences brought me to my knees. I knew I didn't have, and desperately wanted, the deeper awareness necessary to communicate healing and wholeness.

Life has a way of teaching me what I need to learn. It feels good to look back and know that those rough places weren't wasted. Through them I've learned to identify with people who are going through similar problems.

I have had the tendency to treat all people alike—with that big beautiful Sunday morning mask. I simply can't wear my parson's mask any longer and survive with integrity. I think Jesus treated individuals in a unique way. He didn't give pat answers. He looked at every person and started fresh. He gave them a chance to share life. Maybe that's what Christian ministry is all about!

Thanks, Lord, for a job that really has a meaning. I hurt with some of my friends who hate their jobs. They seem to be locked into a role and they may not know how to deal with it. I know that feeling. It's sheer fright to experience those dangerous questions for the first time.

Jesus, your intimate investment in my life enables me to deal cre-atively with my vocation, my calling in life. I want to be able to listen more creatively to my brother and sister who wonder about the meaning of their life-calling.

Unlock me. Help me change and free me up on my job. Provide the freedom and fulfillment I desperately need to be your person in my job.

Thank you for wise and timely guidance for all of us. Help us celebrate wholeness right where we are with all our limitations and potential.

PROPERTY OF
LIVING FAITH CENTER
LIBRARY
SANTA BARBARA, CA.

11

Search for Renewal
in the
Local Church

1. How do you evaluate or describe your search for personal renewal? Can you list three or four periods in your pilgrimage towards personal renewal in your local church? Outside the local church?
2. What does it mean to trust God with your hunger-drive, your longings, your deep desire for personal integration? Who have you known who has spoken to that need most creatively? What happened as a result of your relationship with that person?
3. What are some signs of clear communication in your personal relationships? How do you know when you, or somebody else, is coming through clearly?
4. Are you ready to become a supportive person in your local church? What frightens you when you ask this question? What inspires you? What will such a commitment require of you? With whom might you share such a commitment or experiment in your local church?

11

Search for Renewal in the Local Church

Matthew 23:23-26—*What priorities emerge whenever renewal comes?*
Mark 12:30—*What is the most important priority in the Scriptures?*
Luke 4:32—*Why did Jesus communicate clearly?*
Matthew 7:12—*How do your needs and your gifts relate creatively?*

I experienced approximately four periods of growth in my search for personal renewal. *First,* I met some people who communicated Christian freedom. Whenever I was with them I felt closer to God, I felt more in love with myself, and I sensed the solidness of reality. These people didn't hide their humanity. They celebrated God's grace in the midst of their imperfections, and they encouraged and affirmed other people.

Second, this stirred me deeply and enlarged a conscious awareness for more of the same. I searched the Scriptures and felt a newborn hope helping me get closer to this new experience.

Third, it became more and more clear that this was the way for me. I often prayed a prayer (actually, it's a book title) by Sam Shoemaker, *Revive Thy Church Beginning With Me.* I knew I had to take the plunge first. For months it seemed as though I stood on the razor's edge. I was afraid to launch ahead. It was soon quite obvious that key people in my congregation, and most of my clergymen friends, shunned this new lifestyle that smacked of personal vulnerability and relational sharing. On the other hand, it was even more frightful to turn back and walk away from it. I knew I couldn't do that because things were too staid and lifeless back there. "Oh God," I cried out in my misery, "I'm making a mess of it all, trying so hard to put it together. Here, you take it. Teach me how to trust you, no matter what others feel about me."

That was a hard prayer to verbalize. But I had to pray it because I wanted and needed spiritual and emotional wholeness *more than anything else in the whole world*—and I had to admit this to myself and to God. Immediately following those prayers-of-expectation, I became aware of an opportunity to experience that for which I prayed.

Fourth, God gave me a permanent friendship with someone who loved me and held me accountable in my growth. I didn't know it at the time but now I see this was indeed an answer to my prayers. Ray Wedaa was a layman who knew how to listen without manipulating. I was terribly frustrated with my own ineffectiveness, especially in relating to people on a one-to-one basis. I had all the theological and psychological jargon but *I didn't know how to help people*. I had remained aloof and religious for so long that I could not become vulnerable with the laity—and *be a person* with them. I didn't know how to let me be known to them.

When I first met Ray, I knew he had something I needed. I was somewhat frustrated because he was a Presbyterian, not a Methodist like myself, and I had to drive twenty or thirty miles to see him and sometimes that was an inconvenience. But I knew I needed to learn from and with him.

I made it ridiculously difficult for him. I suggested that he come to my home for breakfast—at 6:00 A.M. By golly, he came. I was sure he would soon give up like all the others, but not so! "Hal, I'd like to meet with you once a week from now on."

I didn't say it, but inside I felt, "I really don't want to get up this early and have breakfast here, and I can't afford to pay for my own breakfast at a restaurant!"

"Ray," I said, "I simply can't afford to go out to eat. I need what you've got and I'd like very much to meet with you at your convenience, but it'll have to be some time other than at mealtime."

"Hal, will you let me take care of that?" Ray responded. "You see, we laymen want to have the chance to minister too. I'd count it a privilege to take care of your meal each week. It would be easier for me to meet you near my office at lunch time. If you could drive over to Wayne's Restaurant I could meet with you every Tuesday. I need you just as much as you need me, and I'd like very much to cover the expense. Will you let me do this?"

I learned over the next six years how much Ray and other *laymen* helped each other in depth. I listened and became known, too.

I saw him give others the freedom to share and be themselves without being criticized and moralized. I noticed how these people related with simplicity and forthrightness and sensitivity. I saw Ray model a quiet, contagious spiritual discipline. He didn't have a college degree. He wasn't a man about town. He was (and is to this day) a businessman with a regular job. And he consistently helps people through toward wholeness!

I WANT WHAT YOU'VE GOT

Imagine what an impact this one man had on my life! During the first year with Ray I saw more people come into a living hope than ever before in my life! I knew there had to be a more realistic way to help people! My hopes were growing. The more I saw the more I hungered for more! I knew I was on the edge of something special. I gradually began to feel very good about being myself. This was a pleasant surprise! I even became joyous that I was in the Christian ministry after all! It felt good to be me, and it felt good to be a clergyman!

However, sometimes I still found it very difficult to prepare for the next Sunday's message. Even after hours of preparation I wondered if what I preached would make a difference.

I remember one particular Saturday morning when I was at the bottom of the barrel, bouncing around in my own self-pity, wondering if I'd have anything worth saying. I picked up Keith Miller's *The Taste of New Wine* and flipped through it quite nervously. I stopped at the chapter, "A Life With Prayer." It was perfect timing. Something clicked inside. As I read how Keith became honest with God and confessed, "God, I'm not so sure I want to do your will!" I found myself saying, "Yes! Yes! That's me! God, I've got to be honest with you. I have those ugly feelings. Darn it! I don't want to do your will either. I don't like what's happening to me. Something's all torn up inside and I hate it . . . I even wonder if I hate you!"

I wept, but kept praying exactly what I felt. Gradually I felt wonderfully cleansed and a sense of inner release. There was a level of acceptance and forgiveness I'd *never* known before. I *felt* what I had read about for years.

"God," I confessed, "thank you for taking all my guff. Thank you for being bigger than my stupid little prayers. Thank you for the freedom to be honest with my own feelings here, now, before you. Thank you for forgiveness! I feel all washed out inside. For once I don't feel like a phony do-gooder who tries to do better or try harder! This is me. I'm for real, and I've just given you what's really inside. And you've listened. You've absorbed my resentment. My stupid, warped image of you is changing. I'm letting a few things out of the bag. Thank you, Father. Thank you for knowing all along what's been inside of me. Thank you for giving me this opportunity to vomit it all out and deal with it."

I walked to church early the next morning with a song in my heart and a message to share. I felt full of God's life and a part of the whole universe. The Scriptures became astonishingly alive. I was amazed at the presence of creative reality all about me. I couldn't wait to share it with my people.

"Father," I whispered to myself, "something is happening to me. Thank you for giving me the opportunity to share. Set us free to be your people during this time together."

I stood behind the lectern and shared this experience in a church school class of about fifty adults—most of whom were leaders in the congregation. I certainly didn't expect what happened. Two spontaneous responses came forward. One elderly gentleman stood up immediately "Why, in all my entire life I never expected to hear a *man of God, a minister of the Word,* say such irreligious hogwash. I am

THIS IS DISGRACEFUL. . . . THIS IS GREAT! WHOOPEE!

stunned. I can't understand why so many of you younger Christians have to go through things like this. I think this is a disgrace."

Another man stood up and said, "Whoopee! I never thought I'd hear a clergyman be so honest. You're the same as I am. I have those thoughts, too. I'm glad you need God like I do!"

Some people were angry. Most of them said nothing. Several came up to me or called during the week to share something personal in their own lives.

Southern California was never so beautiful. I knew I had stepped into a new personal era. For the first time in my life I didn't care what happened to me in the institutional church. I wasn't afraid to be *me*. From that day on my prayer life took on a different tack. I found myself trusting God with a new bunch of feelings! God got bigger and I experienced new dimensions of acceptance. I, too, became a needy person for whom Christ died—not *just* a clergyman giving out the goodies to others. I felt freer to be, to serve, to act.

By far, the most influential ministers in my life were non-clergy. However, two or three clergymen must be added to this list. A senior minister, with whom I worked for four years, listened, prayed, and affirmed me into new dimensions of fulfillment. Phil taught me how to listen because he listened. I was a burden to him at times, but my growth was his greatest reward. I attended several ashrams and experienced the person of E. Stanley Jones. His devotional books, especially *The Way, Christian Maturity* and *The Word Became Flesh,* gave me strategic insights and philosophical handles which helped me understand the basic theological reasoning regarding the relational (or incarnational) Christian lifestyle.

I kept a sharp eye out for clergymen who celebrated the reality of renewal! I met Sam Shoemaker, an Episcopalian clergyman, and knew immediately this man was about the real work of the church! I wrote to him and we carried on a regular correspondence until his death. His letters brought good news. I'm sure his ministry to me through personal letters gave me the motivation and sensitivity to enjoy the ministry of letter writing today. I asked him what he thought was most important in Christian education. (At that time I was minister of education in a large downtown church.) His response to that question will always serve as a major priority in my ministry: "I think there are two things to keep thinking about all the time. One is the everlasting individual, helping him through to a real experience of Christ; and then the kind of small groups where gradually people come to the place where they can be honest, and before that there is increasing love and fellowship . . . education apart from experience is nothing in the Christian life. It has no place. Jesus did not take a dozen men off into some Socratic seclusion and wrestle with their minds. He threw them into the midst of life and acted himself, and let them participate with him. That's a very different kind of education. Actually, I think a great deal of the church's educational program is on a totally false basis, as if merely knowing facts would do anybody any good by itself. This is simply not enough."

Over and over again I thought about Sam's words. "How could I develop a Christian education program with priority on small groups?" I asked myself. It wasn't as hard as I imagined. In fact, the laity wanted it to happen. (How many times I've learned that I was often too far behind the vision of the laity!) So I put Sunday school teachers together in groups and spent time with personal needs as well as Sunday school programs. We prayed together. We became persons together. A sense of community and commitment and mutual trust emerged over a period of months and years.

To my surprise I learned that laymen in my own church wanted to

bless and support me as a person. Al Naito, for example, one of
the laymen in our congregation, became sensitive to one of my needs.
"Hal, how do you like scrambled eggs?" he asked one Sunday
morning. "What do you mean?" I returned. "I'd like to meet with
you every Sunday morning for an early breakfast and give you a
chance to run through your sermon with me—and I'll pray with you."

I took him up on his offer. I wanted the weekly support and accountability of a small group who would, with me, become part of
the proclamation.

Scrambled eggs and scrambled sermon-sharing became the menu
for early Sunday morning. Every Sunday Al showed up. Sometimes
one . . . two . . . six other laymen would attend. We talked about
the sermon. I was frightened at first and did not want these laymen
interfering with my masterpiece. As we grew closer and developed a
beautiful appreciation and trust for each other I noticed that I no
longer felt alone in the pulpit. Sometimes, during a sermon, I'd be
preaching along and glance over at Al and instantly I felt his wonderful support. Sometimes he'd smile or nod his head. What a gift to have
lay people like that!

Needless to say, people noticed the difference in my preaching.
"Hey Preacher, you aren't preaching *at* us anymore. You're coming
through right where we are," several commented. From the first Sunday morning breakfast on I didn't feel alone or judgmental in the
pulpit. Over the years I've consistently initiated supportive prayers
and conversations with at least one lay person prior to a preaching
engagement. These caring, insightful persons help me surrender so
God can work and speak the Good News among the people.

Lay witnessing became a vital part of our worship services. Sunday morning worship became a celebration. We came expecting God
to do a special thing in our congregation.

Even the announcements became fun—and even inspirational.
"Who can spend an hour a week driving Mrs. Lucy Brown, our blind
neighbor, to the doctor?" someone may announce. "Here's a family
without food. We need to get a week's supply of food to them by
tomorrow. What can we do about it?" Someone would respond, "Let's
leave the sanctuary open this afternoon for those of us who'll bring
food for these people."

Specific prayers for loved ones, social problems, or special needs,
were voiced and immediately the congregation would join together
and surround these situations with prayers in the worship service.

It was not unusual to hear someone disagree with the sermon, or interject fresh insights that tied the entire morning message together. I'll never forget a certain dear woman who came to our worship service for the first time. When I asked for spontaneous responses she stood, with tears streaming down her face. The sanctuary grew still while everyone waited until she gained enough composure to verbalize her feelings. "I need to express what's happening to me this morning," she began. "I've never been in this sanctuary before. When I walked into this place I felt a great love within this congregation. I'm really overwhelmed by love! Worshiping a God of love is new for me. I grew up with rigid, religious parents, and church was never a celebration like this! It feels so good to know that there is love like this!"

I addressed our new friend. "Friend, the love you feel here this morning is our gift from the Holy Spirit who lavishes his presence and healing power in the midst of searching people. This can happen to God's people whenever we celebrate his grace and call upon his Spirit."

Now I'd like to share something about the people who had a difficult time with me. They need to be heard and understood. They are not altogether at fault. Over the years the church has trained some of our "old guard" members to be impersonal . . . unpersonal. We have no one else to blame but our own lack of obedience and fellowship within the church.

For years we've believed the old wives' tale that the pastor is to care for the spiritual needs of the church; laymen are the trustees of the material properties and responsibilities. I came to the place where I had to ask myself, "What is my role? What is my responsibility? Do I remain permissively 'patient'? Do I help set new priorities? How do I communicate what the deeper and more personal work of the church is about? If I remain permissive and passive I'll never be a part of a place where people are freed up. On the other hand, if I suggest changes I'll offend some key people in this church! And I know some of those who are the most uptight are paying a good bit toward the mortgage on the new building I've inherited."

The church was located right across the street from a junior high school. The kids were always causing havoc. Windows were broken; fire extinguishers were emptied on our padded pews; twice flour and salt and sugar were strewn throughout the sanctuary. Incidents such as these drove the trustees up the wall. "We must build a fence around the church property. We cannot tolerate vandalism," was their strong reaction. These men spent many hours keeping up the church property. It was costly enough to manage things without teen-age vandalism.

I decided to attend the upcoming trustee meeting. I listened for nearly two hours. Then I said, "Gentlemen, the day you or anyone else spends a penny to build a fence around this property, you can find yourself a new pastor. This place is for kids, too. Once they know it they'll have a different attitude about the upkeep of the property. You, the leaders of this church, must make a choice. Either the church property *or people* come first. One has to give way to the other. I want you to know that I do not justify any vandalism. I do not like what these kids are doing and am totally against it. But *how* we go about responding to the situation is important! So long as I'm pastor of this church we will put the deeper needs of people first . . . and that may mean more than protecting ourselves from a few broken windows!"

A few days later I drove up to the church and found at least a hundred kids standing around a patrol car. An irate adult, a junior high school youth, and a patrolman were in the center of the circle. The patrolman walked over to me. "Reverend, we've got a problem. This boy here broke into the church and I caught him. His dad was called from work. We are waiting to talk to you."

I had seen Steve many times. He got his kicks by beating up other kids. The back end of the church property served as a good fighting place. This time Steve got caught. "Reverend," his father demanded, "this boy has gone far enough. *You* prefer charges and I'll make sure he's put where he belongs. He's always up to no good, he ain't no 'count. *This time I want you to do something!* I've tried everything, Reverend, there ain't nothin' I can do anymore."

I called the patrolman off to a side. "If you'll give me custody of this young man I'll make sure he spends two hours with me each week for six months, on my terms; I'd like to try."

"Okay," he smiled. "Mr. Brown, would you and Steve step into the church office so I can speak to you and the Reverend?"

We sat down in my study. The young man was broken, embarrassed and quiet. The father was glowering with anger. "Okay, Reverend. Please tell Mr. Brown what we're going to do," the patrolman said.

"Mr. Brown, I'm not going to prefer charges on Steve. Instead, we're going to arrange a type of parole program. If you will see to it that Steve spends two hours a week with me for six months, I will work with him on that arrangement and see what we can do."

"Preacher, if that boy misses one time with you I'll make him wish he was never born!"

I dismissed the patrolman and the father. The boy and I sat there. He had no idea what would happen next. It was obvious that he was afraid of me. He'd never been inside a Protestant church. I came over and sat down beside him. After a few long moments of silence I quietly asked, "What do you think of your dad?"

"I hate him. He doesn't know how to handle me. He's never home."

"How'd you like a milkshake?"

He turned his head and looked me square in the eyes. "Yeah, that'd be just great," he smiled. We enjoyed that milkshake and dozens more after that. Weeks and months passed. Steve's grades went up. He joined the baseball team. He became the best pitcher on the team! The principal told me that Steve had changed more than any other youth in the entire school. The story got around the church and the trustees did not bring up the fence-building agenda again.

WHAT KINDS OF FENCES ARE WE BUILDING AROUND OUR CHURCHES?

Renewal was happening! Laymen initiated programs and strategies I never thought possible. The men started a group out on the patio near the garbage cans and delighted in their official church school class name: The Garbage Group. Men who never came to church started showing up in The Garbage Group. Beautiful personal ministries evolved through The Garbage Group. Church became a place where people stopped long enough to care and listen.

Nothing has been more exciting to me than to be a pastor among a turned-on laity. *But something was still lacking.* I was still too busy, and there was that gnawing loneliness inside. I still did not fully know how to let other people minister to my deeper needs. I was caught in a lop-sided lifestyle. I didn't know how to let others into me. "Lord," I prayed, "now teach me how to receive. It's frightening but I'm really ready to let a deeper level of renewal happen to *me!*"

Lord, you've shown me time and time again that I cannot give what I haven't received. For so long I've tried to change others first. I'm too tired and too wise to keep that game going. I've been failing at it for so long. Maybe I'm learning.

Thank you for release! Thank you for a new view. Thank you for the wonderful and frightening freedom to discover the possibility of inner renewal. And thank you for the astonishing freedom that releases me from the constant need to nudge others.

It's so hard to change from an authoritarian role into a sharing style. But it feels so creative and so good to belong . . . and to participate in a mutual caring within a community.

We don't have to be so lonely. I'm making another decision by your good grace, to belong. Catch me again. I'm jumping in heart first.

12

You Need Me?
I Need You!

1. Where are you most distraught in your personal relationships? Have you become known-in-love with that particular person with whom you are distraught? How did you become known?
2. Is it hard to ask for what you really want and need? Why?
3. What does "witnessing" mean to you? How can you enjoy a deeper meaning of *witness*? Are you ready to explore new possibilities?
4. Have you helped people without allowing them to help you where you really need them? What happened to those relationships? Did you feel isolated? Why? Why not?

12

You Need Me? I Need You!

Philippians 2:2—How important is it to have clearly defined commitments and goals in your life . . . in your group?
John 1:14—How close has God come to us? What do we experience in the closeness of his coming among us?
1 John 1:1—Why is God's message one of life and light? To whom?
Matthew 26:37–38—How viable is it to stand alone without the support of others?

The choice was mine. "Should I be known or should I play a role that seems, on the surface at least, to be a rather satisfactory game?" I thought to myself: "Self, you're learning how to get out of the way so your laymen can minister more effectively. But *don't* rock the boat. Self, you will surely get into trouble if *they know* what's really going on inside! Just keep cool, don't get too personal. Self, you've already changed a lot of things. Don't go overboard!"

Fantasies like these raced through my mind. I didn't want to undo anything that provided a place for wholeness. I was fearful that if I let laymen into my *real* life they would reject me. I doubted their ability to keep me afloat. I was saying all the words, but I found it hard to trust the very thing I proclaimed Sunday after Sunday—the priesthood of all believers. Actually, I didn't believe I would be loved and respected if people knew the real Hal Edwards!

I rationalized "I trust Ray. He's twenty miles away. It's better to share my inner life with him because he's not a member of my own church."

At that time I was involved in Faith-at-Work ministries throughout Southern California. The people in Faith-at-Work knew more about

I'M SAYING THE WORDSsss . . . THE WORDSsss

me than my own people. I encouraged a lay-oriented program in my
local church but I didn't put my own life down beside a few people
who were at the heart of the congregation. I did that *somewhere
else!* At the same time, the church was growing, money was coming
in, and attendance grew steadily. New people assumed key leadership positions in the congregation. Finally I had to deal with my own
need regarding deeper relationship to a few key people in my parish.
I talked to Ray. "I agree," he affirmed. "Unless you go back home
and let those people know you, there will be a communication gap.
Yes, I know it's risky. But maybe that's the only way to go."

Through the support of a few people like Ray I slowly let myself
open up to some people in my own congregation. Six of us started
meeting together at 6:00 A.M. every Wednesday. Before we met for the
first time, I shared some personal things about myself with every man
individually. I explained my personal need to belong to them on a
deeper level. I wanted them to know me, to help me grow as a person. I needed some brothers at the heart of the church structure—
people who would make me accountable, who would help me un-

ravel, dream and pray, and live out something worth sharing with others. Every man responded to my invitation. We met weekly. At first it was stodgy and sometimes dull, but we kept edging along until we experienced unity in a common community. After breakfast we would often gather in a circle. One man at a time stepped into the center. We embraced the brother and told him what he meant to us. We held him and recommited our lives to him. Once when it came my turn, I was simply overwhelmed. The strength and warmth of their arms . . . the simple depth and power of those conversational prayers . . . the insight and supportiveness! "Thanks," I smiled through my tears, "You'll never know what it means to be held and . . ." I caught my own words and retracted my statement. "Yes, you *do* know! It's happening to all of us. I don't feel alone anymore."

This was one of several similar incidents which occurred about that time. It seemed that the more conscious my need to be vulnerable became, the more opportunities presented themselves.

Two members, Wayne and Carol, made an appointment to visit with me one Saturday morning. Everything went wrong that week. Several important priorities fell on my head and I was under the pile! The youth program needed help. The choir was unhappy about something. My sermon preparation was tedious and uninspiring. I hadn't been home all week with my family. I didn't want to give myself to anybody. And in they came for an hour of pastoral counselling! And to top it all off they started off with, "Hal, two Sundays ago you mentioned that you wanted us to be honest with you."

That did it! I curled into my shell and waited for the punch line, smiling and looking straight into Wayne's eyes as he continued talking. "Carol and I have something we need to talk about. Remember before we joined the church? You spent time with us. We grew spiritually and we had something to give. It was just great. Then, just as soon as we became members we volunteered to teach the Sunday morning youth class. Now that we've found our slot, it seems that you've forgotten us. I guess we need to tell you that we feel resentful towards you."

That caught me flat-handed. I didn't know how to respond so I let Pandora's box fly open. Tears came. I just sat there like an idiot. I started talking before they had a chance to spoil it by apologizing unnecessarily. "I need you two *now!*" I blurted out. "I'll give you another time when you can get help from me, but right now I need help from you. I hope you'll stay and listen carefully."

YES, I THINK I HEAR WHAT YOU'RE SAYING

"I feel very distraught," I confessed. "I feel like I'm under a mountain of stuff. I feel inadequate, stupid, and undone. I'm hopeful that you will just listen to my feelings and stay with me. I'm quite afraid, but I'm determined to get this out with someone—and I'd like you to help me."

For the next half hour I talked to Wayne and Carol about me. Things came out that I never imagined I'd tell people in my own church. They listened and loved me into a new realm of wholeness— a wholeness I'd never experienced before with my own people. Toward the end of the hour I found myself saying, "I apologize for taking your time," and immediately I laughed and explained my laughter. "For the first time in my life I understand . . . I finally understand why laymen apologize to me for taking their time! It's hard to ask for help when you really need it, isn't it?"

They held my hands as we prayed. Wayne prayed first. Before that time they'd never prayed out loud. "Lord," he prayed, "we came to Hal for help, but he needs our help. We can't understand how we've helped him, but we can sit with him and listen and be his friend. Maybe that's what he really needs. We aren't sure. But we thank you for touching Hal where he needs to become more alive. Help him change. And help him know that we're receiving more than we ever dreamed we'd get this morning.

"Hal let us see him as he really is, and in seeing him we've found You, too. Amen."

I've thought about that prayer many times since then. The words "and in seeing Hal as he really is we've found you" kept haunting me. I read and reread the first few verses of John's Gospel and it finally dawned on me. I was stumbling into relational (or incarnational) Christianity! The more I studied the meaning of "witnessing" the clearer it became. In my vulnerability with Wayne and Carol, and in my new surrender to Jesus *in their company,* I was a witness! I didn't tell them *about* Jesus. I did not lay something religious on them. *I went through something with them* and we all experienced a new relationship with God in the process.

God gave Betsy and me the rare privilege of knowing Bill and Jane. They attended our church almost by accident. They said they had attended many churches in the area and ours was to be their last try. But, as they told me later, their curiosity was aroused when we were talking about surrender.

When I first saw Bill it was as if I already knew him intimately. Our inner spirits reached out to each other with immediate joy. I wanted more and more to be with these people. Their search was intolerably magnetic.

The four of us spent lots of time together and the wee hours of morning came all too soon as we shared. Growth is sometimes painful, often too painful to admit. Sometimes I wonder if all my religious training was a stumbling block, because these two people in their honest searching pulled everything I had learned apart, piece by piece. I searched my soul many times as we sat together.

We'd talk about bullfights and shoot billards together. Bill would say, "Why weren't you an engineer? It would be much easier if you weren't a preacher! Then we could be friends without this religious God-bit getting in the way."

Then he'd stop, smile, and quietly say, "I guess if you were an engineer I'd still have to deal with God, wouldn't I?"

Our struggle in the faith and our struggle with communication brought us together in a mutual friendship. I needed to be unlocked and set free in my personal relationships. God ministered to me through this couple! Bill also grew up on the assumption that wholeness comes by doing good, serving others, and trying harder. He had to reject this in order to find Jesus. He struggled openly and honestly with us regarding his faith. In his struggling I had to reexamine my own faith.

Eventually it was Bill who started The Garbage Group back on the church patio. It was Bill who helped strangers feel comfortable. It was Jane who taught and touched junior high school kids and helped them celebrate. These two people brought new hope into my life and into our congregation. Little do Bill and Jane know what an impact they made on us all. God really has a sense of humor! He keeps coming. He continually teaches us what we need to learn, whether we want to learn it or not! Sometimes he uses the most improbable people. He upsets me so he can set me up again—for *new things.*

I shall never forget a particular Thanksgiving Day. For some reason I was down and didn't feel thankful at all. I was depressed and wanted to run away, but I had to talk to a hundred and fifty people about the joy of Thanksgiving! "God," I said, "what do I do? I'm not feeling very thankful now. You know how I feel and I know I'll probably telegraph my real feelings to all those people. I can't play games with you or myself. What do I do?"

I shared this experience with the people and told them about David who admitted his true feelings in the Psalms. I admitted that I was so swallowed up with my own problems that I didn't feel grateful. However, I did find myself celebrating a God who was *always* there, *always* dependable, and *always* real. I invited anyone who wished to stay after the service for a few moments of feedback and prayer. "I need you today. I need your supportiveness and I'd like to work through this with a dozen or so of you who could remain for an hour following the service."

The words came out before I knew what I was saying! Would anyone stay? Twelve people did. We pulled our chairs into a small circle. I knew that Betsy was struggling with some things at home. Living with me at that particular time didn't make things easier for her. I was gone too much and she was saddled with family responsibilities too often. She was trying to reach out and grow, and growth was hard for her too. Both of us shared in the group. When Betsy started talking she burst into tears. I couldn't minister to her at all. I was locked in. Bill walked across the group and held her in his arms. It was beautiful to see my wife held in the arms of such a community of caring people. Needless to say, Thanksgiving Day became real in that holy moment. That experience brought Betsy and me into new personal growth.

God took a few laymen and converted me because I let them into my life and ministry. They consistently help me work through and understand my fears. They've shown me how people can lead each other toward wholeness. They free me from the bondage of religious and verbal rigidity. They bring me out of a program-orientation toward a more practical program for people. They are teaching me how to *listen others into significance*. They are constantly validating the power of an enabling ministerial style.

I no longer see myself as the authority, the man out front. I feel most creative when I function as one of the members of the body— acknowledging, celebrating, and experiencing the gifts of others.

Jesus, you didn't want to go it alone, either. You asked for supportive friends. Sometimes they didn't hear your cry for companionship and caring prayers.

I can identify with Peter and James and John. Sometimes I'm so bound up in my own problems I can't hear the hurt of others who need me nearby. I simply pass people by and leave them in their pain. I do that most often with people whose pain I cannot identify with.

Maybe one of your great gifts to us is your need for supportive fellowship.

Maybe I do cheat you when I forget that you need me to stay close to you through a hurting brother or sister. Is that what love's about? I know I need other people. I can't be free alone. Maybe you do need my love. Maybe it's you loving us through each other when we stay nearby.

13

Did I Commit Institutional Suicide?

1. Is the Body of Christ synonymous to the institutional church? Does Christ call us to his body or to the local church or both? What is the meaning of your commitment to the church?
2. Are you joyous or fearful about the changes taking place in your church? What do you want to see your local church doing? What red tape keeps you from participating freely? What do you like most about your local church?
3. Do you believe the church is in a time of reformation, revolution? Why? Why not? How do you fit into where the institutional church seems to be going from your point of view?
4. What three questions would you like your local congregation to struggle with? What's the best way you know to introduce these questions and allow a creative process to emerge? How can everyone be involved and have a part in the process? Where do you start?

13

Did I Commit Institutional Suicide?

Matthew 16:15–19—*What's the most important question you'll ever ask or answer for yourself?*
Colossians 3:14–15—*What will give you the freedom to experience more gratitude?*
Revelation 3:1–3, 8, 15–17, 20–22—*What's God saying to the church you belong to?*
1 Corinthians Chapter 12—*How do you see the Body of Christ in your community today? Where do you fit into that body?*

"Why leave the local church? Why switch vocations at a time like this, when things are finally breaking through? What will my people think? What will my bishop say? Am I making a stupid decision? Can I be effective outside a prestructured system? Will I be disloyal to my call to preach?"

This episode begins on November 13, 1968. I was taking a shower. A quiet little fantasy conversation started between the Lord and me.

"Lord, thanks for this place. Thanks for all you're doing here. I'm beginning to like it here!"

My imagination spoke back, "But what if you are offered something else? Would you leave here?"

I was startled. "Why . . . why not! Just so it's even more exciting than this!" I quipped.

Four days later Betsy and I had a date with our church secretary and her husband, our lay leader and his wife. They arrived at 7:00 P.M. and the phone rang as we started walking out the door.

"There's a long distance call for a Mr. Hal Edwards."

"This is he."

"Go ahead, please."

"Is this Hallelujah Edwards?"

The voice was distinctively Ben Johnson's, and he spent twenty minutes introducing Betsy and me to a new job opportunity in an ecumenical lay renewal movement. He told me about a fellow named Dean Griffith in Chicago and how Dean and some laymen had started a small group movement. He said the movement needed a full-time director. My immediate response was, "Gee, that sounds great, Ben, but I don't think that's for me."

"Hal, if you are for this job and if this job is for you, you'll know it. I'm asking you to be as open as you can. Dean will call you in a couple of days. Will you pray about this and give Dean a chance to talk more about it?"

"Why sure," I said. Betsy and I looked at each other and giggled. It became a joke and we greeted our friends and went out the door. As we backed out of the driveway I started talking. "Folks, I've got the joke of the year . . . I mean *the* joke of the year."

I told them everything Ben had said. Nobody laughed. I was astounded with their immediate response. "It's not stupid at all. It doesn't sound like some far-out joke. We see you doing something like that, Hal. This may be the most exciting and meaningful thing that could happen to you."

I couldn't concentrate on the play. After dinner we went over to our friends' house and sat on their new shag rug and talked for a long time. I shared quite openly and those beautiful friends supported Betsy and me as we worked our way through a bundle of compounding emotions. By this time my head was clogged with new questions.

I went to bed several hours later but couldn't sleep. Betsy and I talked far into the wee hours of the morning. I recalled how, just three or four days earlier, I had this "coincidental" conversation in the shower. That memory served as a small reminder that perhaps God was in on the deal. We prayed together, "Lord, protect us from leaving . . . or staying . . . and please give us enough common sense to know which to do."

A quiet peace came to us and we both relaxed and fell asleep.

All day long the next day my brain felt like an over-programmed computer. A constant flow of questions swept upon me. I couldn't concentrate. My sermon wasn't prepared and I sat behind my desk unable to control my thoughts. The phone rang.

"Hello."

A very familiar voice chimed in, "Is this St. Mark's Mental Hospital?"

"Yes sir, it *sure* is," I wheezed. A personal friend "just happened" to be at the Los Angeles airport. He had a forty-five minute layover. Something told him to call me. He was the *one man* I knew who could speak to my specific needs at that particular time! He had already lived through the questions I needed to ask. I believe it was a providential coincidence.

Two days later Dean Griffith called and we made arrangements for an interview. During the next week I visited with twenty-five key people in our local church. I visited with my district superintendent. This was rather frightening at first because I thought he would negate the whole idea from the beginning. How surprised I was to hear Bill say, "Hal, I've been watching your work, and I believe in what you're doing. This new opportunity in Chicago may be cut out just for you. Let me know how your interview goes and when you return we'll talk more about it."

I flew to Chicago exactly ten days after my conversation in the shower! The interview lasted four hours. The first two hours Dean opened his life to me. He let me know him as a person. He gave me his spiritual and emotional autobiography. Then he asked me to tell him about myself. At the end of those four hours I returned to the airport and decided to make an official decision on the following Tuesday.

The big questions for me were, "Am I willing to trade my security in an established system for a new movement which has no credibility at all in the eyes of the church? Can I take the risk and put a group of laymen in the place of a bishop and district superintendent? What if this falls through? Will I be committing institutional suicide? Will my bishop give me special permission to transfer without injuring my connection to the conference?"

Dean called the following Tuesday. "I want to make it official that we would like to have you come to Chicago and be the Director of Christian Laymen of Chicago."

I was ready to respond to the invitation. "Everything seems to point that way, Dean. We feel a great deal of support from everyone we've talked to. We believe that it's right to go to Chicago!"

Immediately following Dean's phone call I made an appointment with my ecclesiastical superiors. "I'm very sorry you're leaving the local church," my bishop spoke forthrightly as we sat across from his desk, "but your mind is already made up and I want you to go to Chicago and do a job as if you were going to do it the rest of your life."

Ten days later we purchased a home in the Chicago area and two months later we moved from beautiful Southern California to the upper midwest.

My bishop granted me Special Appointment status for two years which means that I was officially appointed, with full connection to the Southern California Conference, to serve as Director of Christian Laymen of Chicago, Inc. I've always been grateful for that gift. This stabilized me emotionally and kept me from feeling completely cut off. I have always felt a great love and appreciation for the church. I cherish my relationship with her. I have not always agreed with her priorities and policies, but I learned quite early in my ministry that the best place to change something is from within. I was, and still am, committed to the strategy which demands that one work with people and earn his right to bring about changes.

During those two months of final transition I investigated and explored possible meanings of my future relationship to the church. "What does church history say to me? What are the inherent dangers? How can this ecumenical movement relate to local churches in cooperative ministries? What basic relationship must we model as a movement in order to reproduce a balanced program? Will our board become a cameo of authentic lay renewal? Will we be partners who truly share *or* just another bunch of impersonal decision-makers?"

I believe that CLC is one of many emerging lay renewal movements today. These lay renewal movements are signs of a tremendous evolution taking place in our country and across the world. People seem to be more ecumenical than ever before. Most laymen simply do not think in denominational terms. The marketplace forces us to cross these fences. Many of us are not so spiritually narrow-minded as we were a dozen years ago. Local churches and seminaries are merging and cross-currents are bursting forth everywhere.

Many believe that the church will become one where it really counts. I believe we must preserve unity and uniqueness. It is my opinion that we'll never come together through doctrinal or political management. I really don't see us coming together except through our common humanity, in Jesus Christ. Every day we witness growth at a grassroots level in these emerging small group movements.

Now, how to harness this inevitable advance is a primary concern for those of us who participate in the renewal process. I find myself

asking questions like: Where am I heading? What shall my relationship be to the established church? What does the very existence of
a movement like this say about the church? How can I utilize my
particular gifts and specific ministries and feed the renewal process?
Will I help CLC establish healthy models and policies that will support the renewal process in local churches? These are questions I
continue to live with.

YOU ARE UNIQUE!

During the past five years I've been involved with people from
many churches, both Catholic and Protestant. I've joined with teams
of lay people who come from every conceivable church background.
Time and time again I see a thing of rare beauty growing, moving,
emerging. I'm convinced that we are standing in the foothills of another reformation. I'm not so sure this reformation will be characterized by laymen and clergy *leaving* the institutional churches or
synagogues. It's my hope and prayer that reform will come from

within. Our dream is that these small group movements will serve well and be a positive renewal force within the emerging church today.

I personally feel that I'm closer to my calling than ever before. My role is not that of a local pastor, but I see myself as a member of a floating parish. We at CLC see ourselves as ecumenical catalysts, specializing in small groups and a variety of equipping ministries so that more clergymen and lay people can have permanent support, creative accountability, and wholesome fellowship in an ecumenical setting.

A few months ago, while attending our annual CLC Board weekend retreat, I read these paraphrased verses from 1 Corinthians, chapter 12. I believe Paul's insight regarding the diversity of the members of the Body of Christ must be foremost in our thinking if we participate in creative lay renewal strategies today:

> Our physical bodies have many different parts, but when they are all put together there is one single body. That's the way it is with the Body of Christ. We are all a vital part of the one body of Jesus Christ. Some of us are Methodists, Baptists, or Catholics. Some of us are in economic or racial bondage. But the Holy Spirit has woven us together into one single body. We all have been incorporated into the body of Jesus Christ. We are brothers and sisters by the one Spirit. We have all been given free access to that same Holy Spirit. Yes, we represent many value systems, traditions, and backgrounds, but we cannot say "I don't need you."
>
> And some of us seem weak and the least important but, in actuality, the weak people are really the most powerful and most necessary. Yes, and we are especially grateful to have some who seem rather odd!
>
> God has put this body together in such an extraordinary way—so that extra honor and care are given to those who might otherwise seem less important. This creates mutual helpfulness among all the people. If one among the fellowship suffers we all experience that suffering; if one among us is honored we all celebrate.

> Each of us are together in the Body of Christ and each person is uniquely essential and gifted. Of course, we have

different gifts. But don't neglect the best gift of all—
something that each of us is given to share—God's Love.

These words had a very special meaning for us at the board retreat. I listened carefully as the group called out and affirmed each
member. We celebrated and named the gifts of each; placed our
hands on each one, and thanked God for his/her uniqueness.

I think CLC's primary reason for existence is to participate in this
sort of ministry. This, we believe, is what the work of the church
should be.

When you and I become free in Jesus Christ, we are able to hear
each other and speak the truth in love. We are equipped to minister to each other, and the sharing of life becomes vital, not merely
verbal.

I believe that God is honoring such a ministry. This is why I took
the risk of trading in my bishop for a committed laity with "a shaggy
dream." I'm glad I did it. I wouldn't have missed it for anything!

*Jesus, what do you look like? How do I know the shape of your
body? What does it mean to touch you? To what, or to whom, do I
commit myself if I'm committing myself to the Body of Christ?*

*I keep hearing your words, "Where two or three . . . or, inas-
much as you've done it to the least significant person around here
you've done it to me . . . or, if I don't love my brother whom I
see here and now how can I love God?"*

*I hear you saying, "Hal, you can't find me except in your brother
and sister. I will make myself known to you in relationship to them.
Go out. Visit them. Clothe them. Feed them. Live it out with them."*

*You know, Lord, it's much better to commit my life to people and
not just to theories and principles and bricks. I'm glad you have a
warm body.*

14

How I'd Prey
and Pray

1. Have you learned how to pray conversationally? How did you come into it? Who taught you to pray effectively? Do you feel that God hears your prayers? Why? Why not?
2. Do you find it hard at times to share your real feelings with God? Have you discovered the prayer of surrender? What happened the last time you opened it all up and gave the load to him?
3. List three books which have helped you get hold of a more meaningful prayer experience. What did these books teach you?
4. When you pray do you find yourself "letting go" with God? Does your voice inflection change? Do you feel phony? Why? Why not?

14

How I'd Prey and Pray

Matthew 6:5–8—What's the advantage of praying with a single-minded focus upon the heavenly Father?
James 5:16—Why is prayer more meaningful after you admit your faults to somebody in the community?
Ephesians 3:14–19—How does God's love shatter preconceived notions?
Romans 15:30—Do you have a dependable prayer-partner? Why? Why not?

Prayer seemed impersonal during most of my early years. The preacher prayed long endless prayers during Sunday worship when I was a child and our family memorized a short table grace. Every night I knelt beside my bed and said "Now I lay me down to sleep . . . ."

I've learned that whenever I get into real trouble I pray with my own words. I want to make sure God knows what I mean. And when I need something special I tell God all about it. But for many years that was the extent of my prayer life.

Prayer is often wanting something from God. It is my way of reminding God that I am insured and he's taking care of me.

When I became an "evangel" I was taught to pray for the souls of lost and dying men and women—people who hadn't found the way. For years I concentrated on *their* salvation. I used prayer as a means of changing other people. I didn't realize I was more interested in changing people than loving them. I wanted them to accept *my* theological sounds. I often wondered why I felt uncomfortable and phony when I prayed so fervently for other people to change. Now I realize that I was *preying on them,* I wasn't praying *with,* or even *for,* them.

Much of my praying has been pure selfishness. Many times I asked the Lord to change people so that I could be theologically comfortable with them. I didn't know much about meeting and accepting people where they were. I was taught to help change a person and then show him God's love. I had it all backwards! I interpreted many Scripture verses to fit my own narrow preying. "Ask for whatever you want . . . . Whatsoever you ask in faith believing it shall be done . . . . Nothing shall be impossible to him who asks in faith."

I see now that I did not understand these Scriptures. I neglected the most important phase of all . . . *"in Jesus' name."* For years I simply overlooked this little phrase.

" 'In Jesus' name'. . . . What does that mean? Does it refer to the way Jesus treated people? Does it point to a quality of communication? Does it bring a given situation into an honest perspective? If

IT'S IN THE BAG. . . . ISN'T IT?

I am to pray 'in Jesus' name' does that mean that my prayer will funnel through his person, his guidance, his ability to balance the situation?"

I thought about this and slowly changed my attitude about prayer. Prayer became less religious and more practical. Praying became an attitude and a relationship—not merely a memorized daily ritual. Praying, I'm discovering, is not talking God into changing others; it's a time to surrender and flow with the Spirit in relationship to others. Prayer is letting my soul free to rest or experience the real Presence within and around me. Prayer is not locking people out. Prayer draws circles around all of us!

One day during an ashram I had the opportunity to take a walk with E. Stanley Jones. I was just out of seminary and quite anxious to test this great man with my ingenious questions. I thought to myself, "If I ask Brother Stanley a deep question he'll probably spend the whole hour answering it. I know, I'll ask him to tell me what prayer is and how it works for him."

We walked during the time designated as Work Hour. He carried a cloth sack over his shoulder and he picked up pieces of stray paper with his stick as we strolled along. "What do you want to talk about?" he inquired.

"Brother Stanley, tell me about prayer," I responded.

"Well, let me see. Kagawa taught me that prayer is surrender, surrender to God. That makes sense. God made the universe. The whole universe is made to God's specifications. When we pray we fit into the universal order of things. Life works when we pray, when we surrender."

I waited for more, but there was only silence. He was a wise old gentleman. He let the silence bounce those thoughts back and forth in my mind.

This concept revolutionized my awareness of prayer! Prayer wasn't just a gimmick to change other people. Prayer is surrendering to Someone who can put the pieces together. Prayer puts broken pieces together! This led me into a personalized prayer journey.

I seldom trusted God with *certain* feelings . . . like anger, fear, distrust, and sexuality. I simply had no concept of creative prayer when these feelings first emerged. So I'd pray, "God, take these things away. Free me from these feelings so I can serve you better."

I think a lot of my prayers are still quite naïve. Sometimes I am afraid to let God really deal with all my feelings! After all, he might disapprove of me if I let him know those feelings! Several years ago my attitude about prayer was stretched once again when I read Malcolm Boyd's *Are You Running With Me, Jesus?* I saw myself in that book of prayer. Michael Quoist's *Prayers* enlightened me. I learned that I can communicate with God about anything anywhere.

A friend remarked how I was changing. "Your prayers are different. You used to pray at us; now you're coming through because you're talking to God in everyday language. I find it much easier to talk to God now because you've changed."

Gradually I started telling God exactly what I felt about him—even when those feelings were negative and self-centered and ungrateful. By giving him that part of the real me I discovered new feelings of acceptance and new freedom to praise him! He did not strike me down. He did not chastise me. He absorbed my fear and distrust and melted me in the warmth of his solid acceptance.

My image of God has changed as a result of these new insights and experiences. God's so much bigger and wiser than I ever dreamed. He isn't shocked by my stupidity or selfishness.

Sometimes when I talk with people who are just beginning to pray I suggest these four steps of Ros Rinker's. They are: 1. Jesus is here. 2. Thank you, Lord. 3. Help me. 4. Help my brother or sister. *Jesus is here*—I can begin by acknowledging his real Presence right where I am. *Thank you, Lord*—celebrate. Together we express our gratitude. Gratitude, we discover, opens doors for new opportunities. Thanksgiving is usually the healthiest and most realistic response I can express. *Help me*—Lord, I'm not putting the pieces together very well. I need help again. I'm not what I want to be. Enable me to be the person I need to be in this situation. Guide me. Fill me. Help me. *Help my brother or sister*—I'm aware that Jim may be suffering because of our broken relationship. Surround us both with special guidance. Give us sensitivity and perception. Enable us to be part of the answer to my prayer, and restore us to You and to each other.

There is another simple prayer format, not unlike Ros Rinker's steps. They are built around the word ACTS. *Adoration*—Tell God the good things I know about him. Praise him. Celebrate his power and love and grace. *Confession*—Admit to God what's wrong. Share real needs. Own up to specific imperfections, desires, misgivings. *Thanksgiving*—Celebrate the way God forgives and understands. This is a time for sincere expression of personal appreciation because God continues to show great love and solidarity in the midst of our imperfections. *Supplication*—honest concern for others who need support and God's particular guidance and help.

Origen was one of the early devotional masters in Christendom. He lived from 185–254 A.D. He wrote hundreds of years ago: "It seems to me that four subjects (of prayer) . . . may be outlined . . . At the beginning *God is to be glorified* through Christ . . . in the Holy Spirit . . . And next in order *general thanksgiving* including blessings bestowed on many besides himself, together with those blessings he has personally obtained from God. After thanksgiving, it seems to me that he ought to accuse himself bitterly before God of his own sins, and then ask God, first for healing that he may be delivered from the habit that causes him to sin, and secondly for forgiveness of the past. After *confession,* it seems to me that in the fourth place he should add his *request for great and heavenly things for his family and his dearest.* Finally he should bring his prayer to a close glorifying God through Christ in the Holy Spirit."

In each of these three prayer-models we find four basic ingredients: Adoration, Thanksgiving, Confession, Supplication. (Supplication, as I see it, means caring for others.)

Some people think they have to sound like a junior preacher. Others desperately cling to a ritual or written prayer; some of us feel too insecure with spontaneous prayers. I've learned that there are many ways to pray. God knows my heart and he knows my capacity to express myself. But this does not justify my laziness! I *must* learn how to pray so I can participate in the nitty-gritty of the abundant life. Prayer is like breathing. If I don't breathe the resources of God into my daily life I have very little to breathe out to others during the day. Do you find this true?

Fifteen years ago I had the opportunity to sit in a prison cell and hear a young man pray his first prayer of personal surrender. It wasn't the kind of prayer you'd print in a typical church bulletin. He butchered the English language, and his prayer was accentuated with a few four-letter words. But something miraculous happened. The cell was filled with God's glory. There was a glow, a godly glow, in this guy's face. He blew a hole through the ceiling and got hold of God with that prayer! He told God exactly what he felt. His honesty paved the way toward God's immediate gift of himself.

I believe God always answers every prayer. For example, he may answer with a "yes" or a "no" or "wait awhile." Every "unanswered" prayer is nothing more than the goodness of God working without our immediate knowledge. Think how terrible life would be if you and I got everything we asked for—just when we made our request. I know that my own ignorance and selfishness would dominate God's omnipotence! Then I'd block the true flow of life at its best.

I still do not understand why God doesn't answer some prayers—especially those prayers relating to suffering. Sometimes I just tell God off, "Why don't you help so-and-so? You know she's suffered terribly. Why can't you heal her body and relieve her from that impossible situation? How much longer do you expect me to believe in you if you don't heal her?"

I know all the time that this is a game, that God knows how to take care of my friend better than I. I'm also aware of my ignorance of the deeper meaning of healing. I often struggle with my own impatience and lack of faith. I sometimes feel like the father whose child was brought to Jesus. He said, "Lord, I believe (a little bit); help me overcome my unbelief."

If prayer is surrender, as E. Stanley Jones said, then prayer is also celebrating the gifts of God.

I think the Scriptures often provide opportunities to pray. The Scriptures help me clarify my relationship with God so I can actualize my gifts—i.e., put them to work in *practical* ways.

I'd like to think that I can be completely objective and honest *alone* with God, but this is not always true. Guidance often comes when I pray alone. The still small voice does speak and I am blessed, but I've often found it necessary to check out "my guidance" with a supportive family. Three people, or twelve people, usually make me three times, or twelve times, more objective regarding "my guidance" from God. Almost always I am affirmed and encouraged to follow the guidance I receive in private prayer. But now and then I need to be checked by other people. Sometimes the guidance I receive from God is clogged or distorted by my lack of self-knowledge.

When I think of prayer I think of Michelangelo. The story goes that he was rolling a huge piece of granite down a hill into his studio. Someone shouted out, "Hey, what are you going to do with that ugly piece of marble?"

Michelangelo shouted back, "There's an angel in there and I'm going to let him out!"

Sometimes we simply cannot perceive God's set of facts in a situation until we pray. Prayer that emerges from a quiet center "lets the angel out."

I must confess, I cannot praise God for everything that happens, especially when a tragedy comes. Several years ago a beautiful young woman was killed instantly in a car wreck. I attended the funeral. I shook my head as if to say, "No, I cannot agree with you," as the pastor elaborated on God's divine will regarding the death of this girl. "God planned it this way. His ways are far greater than ours. He has planned a great welcome for so-and-so, and we must rejoice that his will is being accomplished. We do not understand it, but we must accept it."

I was sick to my stomach by the end of the sermon. I'm not able to praise God for things like that. I can't lie about my feelings. I would be much more honest with God if I were to tell him how it hurts, and how I don't like what happened. I admit that I don't understand why things like that happen. "God," I remember praying during that funeral, "I don't think you wanted this to happen. I believe you are hurting with us. I know that you *allowed* this to happen, but I don't think you *wanted* it to. Dear God bring something good out of this mess! Teach me how to use this tragedy."

Perhaps you've never prayed with anyone in your life. I suggest that you ask God to help you find a friend with whom you can experiment in conversational prayer. You might begin by using one of the methods suggested in this chapter. At first I suppose you may feel awkward and self-conscious, but don't let that stop you. I felt awkward at first, too. Nothing worthwhile happens without consistent exercise, and that includes prayer. To "pray without ceasing" does not mean that we go around with our eyes fixed on the heavens all day long. It means that God is with us all day long in every situation and we can celebrate his life in us at any given moment. I feel that God wants me to become more conscious of his tremendous ability to live in us. One of my constant prayers is, "Lord, teach me to perceive your life in this specific situation."

The Pittsburgh Experiment introduces people to a "Thirty-Day Prayer Experiment." The experiment challenges people to pray the following prayer for thirty mornings. At the end of the thirty days a person may evaluate the validity of prayer and determine for himself, through specific experiences, if God is for real. This prayer has served thousands of persons, introducing them, through practical daily experiences, into the kingdom of God. You may want to paraphrase your own, or use this one. Pray this prayer out of "unbelief" until you *have* to believe—because of the way God begins to move into your life.

Good morning, God.
Thank You for loving me.
What do You have for me today?
I want to be a part of it.
Amen.

Lord, I've wept and I've laughed in my prayers. I've told you my good feelings and my bad feelings. I've screamed out of pain and danced out of sheer joy. I've been quiet and restful knowing that you are close by.

You keep drawing us out, teaching us to pray. Your Spirit helps us express what we cannot verbalize alone.

Thank you for making prayer possible. How could we feel you otherwise? How could we cope without feeling your breath of life within and around? I think I'd go bananas!

I praise you for the gift of prayer and for your tremendous patience with me when I feel so prayerless.

15

Stages

in the Scriptures

1. What are your first recollections of the Bible? How do you relate those early experiences to your current relationship to the Scriptures?
2. How do you read the Bible? Have you found a style that works for you? When do you find the Bible most helpful? Where do you like to read the Bible?
3. How do you feel about marking your Bible with questions, insights, key phrases, responses? Have you ever purchased a modern version or translation and used it as a workbook?
4. Can you think of one simple verse or any particular block of Scripture that continually speaks to you? Why do you suppose that particular verse means so much to you? What memories are attached? What discoveries? Any negatives attached to it?

15

Stages in the Scriptures

2 Timothy 3:15–17—*Were you taught the Scriptures when you were young? How do you evaluate that input today?*
Psalm 119:105–106—*How is God's message like a flashlight in a dark place?*
Deuteronomy 6:4–6—*What's the most important mandate in the Bible?*
Revelation 20:11–15—*Why will the word of God outlive everything else that is refined away?*

"Sonny Boy, what do you want for breakfast tomorrow?" my grandmother asked. "Ummmm. Can I have a piece of fried chicken and waffles?"

My earliest recollection of the Bible takes me back to a very special breakfast nook. Whenever I spent an overnight with my grandparents I knew we'd have a nifty breakfast . . . and family devotions.

The delicious aroma of a carefully prepared breakfast filled the house. Three plates were set. And sure enough, two pieces of warmed-over fried chicken, left over from the day before, were placed on a little saucer near my plate.

"Sonny Boy, will you help me read the Scripture lesson for today?" my grandmother asked. "You know I can't read," I replied. "I know, but I'll help you. We can do it together. I'll put my finger on a word and say it, and then you can say it after me. Let's begin here. The . . . Lord . . . is . . . my . . . shepherd . . . ."

Those first impressions of the Bible created an image that has life-long advantages. Those early experiences were realistic, fun, personable, and practical.

Then I remember the huge family Bible. Long before I could read I looked at the pictures. There were a few really gruesome pictures, like the plagues in Egypt. And everybody looked very unhappy. The center section with names and birthdates and death notices enhanced my curiosity. It was great to see in writing that I was born!

My first Sunday school teacher also taught me a great deal about the Bible. Mrs. Stroud, one of those lovely and gifted people, gave herself joyfully to little children. She always gave us the feeling that she cared, and that she knew what she was doing. She kept us busy doing something that related to her stories. She'd tell us stories in our own words. We felt free to tell her secrets and ask questions about anything. Every Christmas we participated in programs or plays depicting the birth of Jesus. At other times we memorized parts depicting the teachings, death, and resurrection of Jesus as well as Old Testament stories. I recall the time we practiced so often we memorized each other's parts! Mrs. Stroud had a way of making every child feel important. We all felt as though we belonged when we were with Mrs. Stroud.

The Revised Standard Version was published during my early teens and my pastor gave me a copy. I was amazed to read the Scriptures in words I could understand. That copy of the New Testament created a tremendous appetite for "more" and the Bible became an exciting book. I read through the New Testament when I was fifteen and sixteen, sprawled out on the floor or on my bed with my feet draped over a favorite chair or pillow. I was astonished to discover that the Bible was practical for people my age.

These new thoughts and insights came as a result of reading the Bible alone as a teenager. I associated wonderful freedom and exploration with my Bible reading. Values and relationships were often clarified. Sometimes the Bible helped me understand my parents—why they wanted me to do certain things . . . and why I acted the way I did in certain situations. Reading the Bible did unlock doors in my personal search for meaning and direction.

These things happened before I studied the Scriptures in systematic or doctrinal depth. During those days I read the Bible and applied what I could understand to current experiences.

When I decided to become a minister I knew I had to study the Bible in depth and learn how to communicate the Scriptures more effectively. The first year in college I purchased a chain reference Bible which became my work Bible for four years. I majored in philosophy and religion and minored in Greek and history. Doctrine,

Greek, church history, and Hebrew saturated my mind with new facts about the Bible. I memorized blocks of Scripture. Many times I read the Bible into the morning hours. I wanted more than anything to be a good student of the Scriptures.

One day I had a conversation with a man I admired greatly. "Hal, the most important thing in life is to have your daily devotions," he said with all seriousness. I listened carefully. "If you don't read the Bible and get God's direction for the day you will not be an effective Christian. Many Christians have lost their witness because they stopped having daily devotions. Remember, if you miss them one day you'll know it inside. If you miss devotions two days your family will know it. And if you miss them three days the world will know it—because you'll run out of spiritual resources. Whatever you do, don't ever cheat God by having half-hearted devotions."

I took my friend-hero so seriously I went for years without ever missing a single day. It became a daily duty to perform so God would love me and bless my efforts through the day. For ten long years I performed with this attitude as the motivating factor. Then it became a noose around my neck. I was finally able to talk to someone about my problem. As a result I discovered that daily devotions should not be a duty to perform, but an experiment of faith. "God is not a religious dictator," another friend assured me. "He's really on your side. He wants you to enjoy life and experiment by faith. He can and will use even your failures. He knows you are a human being with many imperfections. That's what grace is all about."

My heart leaped with new expectations as I listened. I didn't want to throw God or the Bible away. I wanted to grow and change and rediscover what I had had when I was a teenager. These new concepts freed me, and I hope I never forget to show my gratitude for the people who introduced me to these new dimensions.

Now, during the second decade of my Christian growth, my devotional experiences have been much more positive and experiential. Even though I now commit myself *daily* to a *minimum* of an hour (fifteen minutes of quiet waiting; fifteen minutes of Scripture reading; fifteen minutes in study; and fifteen minutes journaling), I find tremendous freedom and benefit. It's a *positive* discipline, one that *does not negate*. In fact, it really introduces me to new resources and attitudes that stabilize me.

I refuse to take myself so seriously anymore. Devotions do make a difference. I know that because of twenty years of experimentation. My mind is sharper and more aware. Things do happen when I read the Scriptures. Guidance and encouragement come through those words into my life. The Scriptures must be inspired because they do inspire me so often. But they also embarrass and frighten me. They make me honest with myself, and that's frightening at times. Sometimes when I'm reading the Bible, new insights and objective thoughts often interrupt my own narrow train of thinking. In a word, reading the Bible helps me celebrate the reality of what I am and can be through a higher Power. Reading the Bible helps me surrender more of my life to that higher Power. Reading the Bible takes the load of living off my shoulders and puts it on his. Then I don't have to take myself so all fired seriously! Reading the Bible helps me shout "Whoopee!" in the middle of my mess!

TELL ME WHO I AM AND WHAT I CAN BECOME

I experienced a lot of pain and struggle in my search for a workable biblical knowledge. On the one hand I could not identify with the doctrinally oriented conservative who worshiped at the shrine of right concepts. On the other hand, I could not identify with the existential philosophy that worshiped at the altar of subjective reality and impersonal social action.

At one time in my theological training I was told the Bible was

verbally inspired—word for word. At other times I was taught that
the Bible is no more inspired than Shakespeare. Some professors and
preachers claimed the Bible to be the ultimate authority of God in the
world, the infallible truth. Others claimed that the Bible is merely a
record of God's action in the world. Still others taught that the Bible
becomes the Word once we accept it and assimilate it into our lives.
Time and time again many of my professors belittled those who believed or taught otherwise.

Much of the theological wrangling I've heard in liberal and conservative camps haven't proved to be very practical. I'm not as interested in being right as I used to be. The more I read the Scriptures
the less I need to prove my particular theological position. Knowing
biblical facts simply isn't enough! Listen carefully now before you
hear something I'm not saying. Knowing the Scriptures is essential,
but it isn't enough. I think I can illustrate what I'm talking about
with a verse of Scripture. The Pharisees were very religious; they
knew the Scriptures by memory. They were, in fact, the most knowl-
edgeable holy men in that culture. But Jesus called them to task
regarding their ignorance. "You do not really know the Scriptures—
or the power of God" he said to these scriptural legalists. What he
meant was, "You've memorized the words but you don't live those
words out in your relationships.

"You load people with impossible demands while you sit around
and look so righteous . . . . You block people from getting into the
kingdom because you pretend to be something you're not! You have
all the words but you ignore the really important things—like attitudes, justice, and genuine faith. Oh yes, you give ten percent of
your income to the church, but you aren't realistic people. You look
like beautiful mausoleums. You try to look so saintly but your hearts
are full of hypocrisy and sin."

Nowhere in Scripture does Jesus Christ express anger as he did
with people who knew the Scriptures but did not make themselves
personally vulnerable. I was one of these legalists and didn't know
it. Often, through sheer ignorance, I violated people by quoting certain Scriptures to prove my selfish point of view. When I discovered
my sickness I almost threw the baby out with the bath water. I'm
glad I didn't. I now appreciate the Bible more than ever, and I have
a different reason for reading it. I'm reading it with one eye on grace
and the other on truth. It's a gift now—not merely a duty.

Some people say the Bible is perfectly recorded in every way.
They believe that God superseded human error when the Bible was

recorded. Others believe that the imperfections of humanity are a part of the Bible, just as the human-divine element is in the church. Some people argue that God chose to work through people like ourselves and risk the involvement of human imperfection—which doesn't take away from the miracle of divine revelation. In fact, they say, it validates the miracle. If God could reveal such living truth through imperfect people so long ago, he can reveal his life to and through people like you and me today.

That's really something worth consideration! Forty writers over a period of 1600 years: kings, prophets, and common people. Sixty-six books in all, and the whole thing is unified with phenomenal structure!

I see the Scriptures pointing the human race to history's hitching post—the person of Jesus, the God/man. In the Old Testament people are shouting, "Someone's coming! Someone's coming! He's going to come! He's not going to leave us in darkness. He will deliver us from our plight! God is with us, just wait and see!"

The New Testament celebrates with hilarious applause, "He's here! I told you he was coming. Look! See how God has kept his word! He comes, not with mere words, but in a living human being! He makes his word relatable! God is with us! Yippee!"

The Bible is God's written announcement—Good News—relating to our daily predicament as well as our eternal questions. Let's face it, I'm in trouble and I need help. I simply can't cope with life without implementing Good News from somewhere! I need help and my broken pieces prove it. God, the Scriptures tell us, has made a door in the wall that boxes us in. You and I can·walk out through that door and experience newness of life if we respond to the source God provides. He loves us totally and He abhors anything that prevents us from the best that life offers. This accounts for God's wrath. He hates what hurts you and me.

For me, the Bible is no longer a book of legalism. It's an invitation to life at its highest. It's God's way of inspiring us and revealing himself to us in a most practical way—through Jesus who knows the way to live in us. God has been very honest with us in the Scriptures. He hasn't held a thing back. You and I will do well to study the Bible and digest as much as we can on a consistent basis.

Some of us have found it easy to reject, or neglect, the Scriptures because we had a loveless experience with a significant person in our past who pushed the God-thing down our throats. Some of us neglect the Bible because we do not see it as a book of healing, wonderment, and tremendous wisdom. Some people do not read the Bible because of other reasons—reasons which may be very important and worth hearing out. Whatever your reason for not reading the Bible, I encourage you to cut through those negative misunderstandings and dare to look for new dimensions!

As you begin to experiment and find your own style for personal Bible study, you'll discover that God speaks in unusual ways through his Word. Perhaps you'll suddenly find that you appreciate the Scriptures in a whole new way because they really do reveal God's action at the point of human need. I hope this will be so!

Jesus, I think I'd never have known you as I do if the Scriptures hadn't come along. You become so alive to me at times when I reach through those words to you. And I see myself becoming alive to myself when I encounter you through the Scriptures.

Thank you for the way you unlock prejudice and insecurity and unfaith inside me. Thanks for the power of life that emerges from those words. I know there's no magic in the print . . . in the words . . . but it's quite evident that there is power behind those words because something happens to me when I open my mind and receive the vibrations of your presence whenever I read the Bible.

I can't understand it. Maybe I'll never understand the dynamics. But I do know that your message is a life-changing factor for me.

Most of all, thank you for helping me work through some basic hang-ups I've had about the Bible so I can enjoy the reality of the message more and more.

16

What
Small Groups
Mean to Me

1. Do you belong to a group that really works for you? What makes your group work? What do you think is missing in your group?
2. What do you want your support group to give you? List one or two possibilities.
3. What do you want to give your support group? List three or four possibilities. Are these similar to the above? Why? Why not?
4. How do you see small groups in your local church? What can you do to help start a group? What should you *not* do? Why?

16

What Small Groups Mean to Me

Mark 6:32—*Why is it important to find a quiet place together?*
John 11:44—*How can we go about unwrapping each other without tearing each other apart? What dynamics are involved?*
Acts 2:44–47—*What do you see here that models Christian community? How willing are you to become involved in this kind of commitment?*
Acts 5:42—*Where did the church meet at the very beginning?*

I made a promise to myself several years ago. The result of that promise was to attend as few small group meetings as possible. There were already too many meetings I had to attend out of necessity.

About that time I received a telephone call from a friend. He was a layman who did not attend my church. "Say, I've been wondering if you would like to come to a small group meeting," he said. Immediately every door in my psyche slammed shut! "Ahh . . . when is it?" I reacted, hoping that I already had something on for any night he might suggest. "Oh, *Saturday* night." "Oh gee, I can't. I've got to stay close to home on Saturday night so I'll have things ready for Sunday morning, you know."

Wow! Did I feel stupid! I winced and kept on lying. "Tell you what, if you meet on a *Thursday* night I'll come and join you sometime. Don't change things just for me, but if it so *happens* that Thursday evening works out for the whole group, let me know. I'd love to come."

Thank God for someone who saw through me and kept on loving me anyway! I put that man off at least four times for a variety of reasons. But he kept calling me and he was tremendously patient. I might have missed the greatest experiences of my life if he hadn't kept close to me!

My persistent friend kept calling me. Finally, because I had used up all of my regular excuses, I attended their *Thursday* evening small group. I knew this group was bound to be different because I never met a layman so quietly persistent. "Something must be happening . . . or else this group must be one sick crowd. There's got to be a reason for this kind of durability and excitement!"

I prayed as I drove to the meeting, "Lord, I sure hope this crowd of people are for real. I'm tired of trying."

Most of the groups I had attended were impersonally prestructured and task-oriented. One could zip right on through those and nobody seemed to care. Besides, being a pastor I consciously or subconsciously enjoyed being the authority figure in the group—the man to turn to when extra help was needed. I hated that role but I also enjoyed being at the center of things. So, lots of questions started zooming through my mind as I approached the front door. "Why am I feeling so anxious? It's just a small group discussion with some people I've never met. What if they're a bunch of religious fanatics?"

THAT GROUP WAS LIKE COOL WATER ON A WARM DAY

The door opened and I walked in. Sitting on the floor, in chairs, and on couches were ten new people I had never seen before. My fantasies and fears left me immediately. I sensed an atmosphere of acceptance and warmth. Before I knew it, I was involved with the most instantaneous fellowship of caring, honest, open-minded people I've ever seen in my entire life! It was so real it was unreal. I knew immediately that this was going to be one of my priorities and I felt hopeful that Betsy would enjoy being with me in the group. I felt chains dropping from my emotional arms and legs. I experienced a surge of hope. The pangs of subtle loneliness subsided. Because of my involvement in that group, I began to discover who I was; I experienced and expressed feelings without wondering if I were some kind of nut. I felt consumed by a new sense of freedom and joy. I never before realized the power of a community of sharing people—until it happened to me.

Obviously, this was not the first time I had participated in a small group, but in this one I experienced a new sense of liberation and wholeness.

Small groups are not new. Jesus, being a Jewish rabbi, adopted the ancient custom and gathered twelve learning-followers around him. He did not stand in front of them and lecture. He took them with him and showed them how to relate to people—all kinds. For three years they lived together. He must have spent seventy-five percent of his time with these men. They slept wherever they could find a place to pillow their heads. They took time to relate to the poor and the wealthy. They saw him absorb and understand the hostility of sick minds. They were amazed at the quiet healing power that came from his touch.

He refused to allow people to put him in a superior position. He did uncanny things like wash feet and communicate openly with women. He did not flinch in the face of the religious professionals who scoffed and criticized his authority.

They lived it out day by day. Jesus let himself be known as a person, and by knowing him personally these learning-followers encountered the living God. They were a stumbling crew. It wasn't exactly an ideal K-Group. Jesus did not pick the kind of group participants you or I might pick. He gathered together an explosive, impossible mixture of humanity. There was young John who asked his mother to help him get a neat position. And Simon Peter who reacted in totally unpredictable ways time after time. Political fanatics, members of the establishment, hard-nosed blue collar types, men who expressed doubt, fear, disbelief, and constant amazement . . . this was the first Koinonia Group! Besides all that, one of the members committed suicide!

A group of "normal" imperfect people became God's major target for the most fantastic revolution in human history! After three years of modeling the new lifestyle, Jesus entrusted these same men with the greatest commission given among men. "Go and get people involved in this new lifestyle and you'll receive power and insight— God will do the impossible through you. Go back home and *don't run away.* You'll be filled with the dynamic of the Holy Spirit. You'll be able to communicate this power to all kinds of people" (Acts 1:8 ff.).

And they did! Something happened to these men. This indwelling Spirit of Christ infused that small group and changed the course of human history.

These learning-followers became apostles, or sent-out ones, because they were enabled by the Spirit to reproduce what they had caught from their Master. In the Book of Acts we read about the small groups that started. When three thousand people responded to Peter's sermon, there were a hundred and twenty people who were already through the process. These people met regularly in homes. They celebrated their new life with bread and wine and the house church movement exploded by leaps and bounds.

These groups dispersed across the Roman Empire. Church history boasts her finest hours during these times when small groups of believers shared life together and reproduced the quality of love among themselves as exhibited by the Man of Nazareth and his learning-followers.

As we check back on the history of Christendom, we see renewal movements about every two hundred years. Martin Luther had his "church within the church," a group of men who met regularly with him over a meal. John Wesley grew up in an Anglican rectory where, as a very young boy, he listened to the laity sing and share and become human together. He initiated a small group, although very pious and highly intellectual, during his college days. At the age of thirty-five, he was finally touched in his heart through a small group of sharing laymen, and this turned his life around. He got his heart warmed and he experienced the reality of a personal faith. Thousands of unchurched people responded, their hearts were afire, and a mighty spiritual movement swept across England and America during the late 1700s. Hundreds and thousands of people were caught up in an age of spiritual awakening.

The history of small groups continues. About fifty years ago a young Episcopalian priest was invited to serve at Calvary Episcopal Church, in Manhattan. They wanted a clergyman who would involve laymen in cooperative ministries. They found young Sam Shoemaker in Hong Kong where he was a missionary. He accepted the call and over a period of years God gave him an extraordinary ministry. Two major movements were born through the ministry of those people, Alcoholics Anonymous and Faith at Work. Relational Christianity characterized this unique ministerial style, and the influence of that strategy and lifestyle affects what many of us across the country are doing in contemporary small group movements.

The small group process has played a tremendous part in history. You can understand why I disagree with people who claim that the small group movement is anti-church. Indeed, I would question whether the screwed-down pews, the impersonal worship services, and the constant breakdown of quality communication have validity in a time when people are desperately hungry for identity and relationships.

I do not advocate that you rush out and unscrew your pews and cut out your worship services. Never! We need to come together in worship; through worship we can experience God in community! Needs are met and ministries are born and people are reborn when Good News is funneled through God's ministers, be they clergy or lay. How extremely essential are those pastors and churches who in an hour of worship set men free! How poor we are without them!

Small group sharing is not enough for me. I need to belong to a worshiping people. I would like to believe that some day we will experience the closeness and commitment on Sunday mornings that we usually experience in small group sharing. The Apostolic Church (read Acts, chapters 2 and 3) did accomplish this amazing balance. Somehow we must discover ways to weave small groups *and* worship *and* mission into creative tension. We must listen to God, work together, and develop a strategy in response to his guidance!

What will happen if we do not get it together? There will be factions and unnecessary problems between local churches and movements like CLC. It seems to me that we can help each other rather than compete. Small groups have become a valuable life-line to hundreds and thousands of people in our country. It seems quite apparent that we are currently cresting a wave of opportunity. People—be they clergy or lay—whose lives have been changed by involvement in small groups may not settle for anything less in the future.

I CANNOT BE WHOLE ALONE

The church of the future must incorporate small groups as a top priority or we'll miss out on a valuable person-to-person ministry.

I need a support group because I want to be a whole person. I cannot be whole alone. I cannot celebrate my gifts alone. I do not even know what my gifts are until they are called out and affirmed by supportive people! To tell the truth, I don't know who I am alone. I am one of those people who needs regular times of encouragement and accountability with a few brothers and sisters.

What do small groups mean to me? A small group is a place and a people where I can come to know and love God and myself. It serves as a testing ground for my dreams and insights. A small group surrounds me with enough honesty and enough grace to keep me balanced. A place that lets me belong without having to perform. A small group helps me grow and obey God.

I was in a small group when I first experienced *total* acceptance and love before God. I was in a small group when I learned how to verbalize my need to be a creative listener. Through small group encounters I have been renewed in my personal and family relationships. Because there are supportive people close to me I am learning more about stepping forward into unknown and uncharted places.

Small groups will not be quite as meaningful for some people. There are some who should not get involved in small groups! Some people can squelch a group in no time flat. We must help persons know how to get into a group, how to get out of the group and, most of all, why the group exists in the first place. I've seen groups die a slow and painful death because they did not begin with clear commitments. Some small groups deserve a quick and effective funeral service. This can be done without violating or repressing the history of that group!

Are you in a small group? Do you want to be in one? Scout around. Ask some important questions. Find some people who exude those qualities and characteristics you hunger to share. How will you know them? Jesus said, "Here is how to evaluate it, the greatest love is exhibited when people lay down their lives for each other" (paraphrase of John 15:13).

Where are those pockets of people who meet together in the name of Jesus? By all means, find them and join the fellowship if you want to get involved in a life-changing experience. But, on the other hand, do not get involved unless you want God to make a radical change in your life. Because he really will change you in such a group . . . if you let him and if that group is called into being by God.

Jesus, what can I tell anybody about small groups? I can tell them how I've found real family. I can witness to personal growth and change. I cannot doubt what I see happening to me and others.

You've made me a creature of community. I am a deflated nobody when I do not belong, and small groups have provided a place for me. I see myself progressing when I participate in a supportive fellowship.

I've been in some lousy groups, Jesus. But you understand that better than I. I know, I was part of the problem. Teach me to communicate clearly, simply, and openly in my support group. Make my group a healing station. Help me cope and communicate and serve with power and quality.

Lord, make my group a launching pad from which each of us can flow out into life with effective influence. Keep us from locking the world out. Help me and my support group enter into the whole scope of Christian growth.

17

Jesus and
My Personal
Sanity

1. Do you suppose God might be saying something important to you through the human potential movement? If so, what? How do you connect this with God's providence today?
2. When did you last experience the gift of God's unique presence in a so-called secular setting? What did you learn from that experience?
3. Have you ever felt as though you had lost your senses? Your identity? Your sanity? If so, what happened to you? When, if ever, did you experience any supportiveness? From whom? What happened?
4. How do you relate Jesus Christ to your personal sanity? Is there a definite connection between the two for you? Why? Why not?

17

Jesus and My Personal Sanity

Luke 4:18–30—*What are Jesus' priorities for wholeness and ministry in terms of our behavior and mission?*
Mark 5:1–20—*How many roles—personages—swirl around in you? Can you name a few?*
Luke 19:1–10—*Why did Jesus say wholeness had come to that home? What do you need to do so that wholeness can come into your home?*
Mark 2:15–17—*Are you on the inside or the outside while the party is going on? How do you identify with this story?*

Jesus has a way of touching and teaching people and making them whole. He consistently engages in the sacrament of touching. He touches people spiritually . . . physically . . . emotionally. He heals thought-patterns, bodies, and emotions. Jesus has no hang-ups regarding sexuality. He has the ability to communicate in a unique way to every individual he meets.

For two thousand years men have studied the lifestyle of Jesus. Do you ever wonder how he could make so many people whole in such a short span of time? If the New Testament record is true, Jesus revealed truth and reproduced wholeness. People were different after he came into their lives. They were unwrapped from years of pain. They were liberated to be themselves. They learned how to deal with their past and express gratitude. They were given new eyes to see themselves and the world about them. They became saturated with the Good News that sets people free. The brokenhearted were able to use their pain. Captives were released from prisons—oftentimes prisons within—where years of anxiety, hurt, or hostility isolated them from relatives and neighbors. They were fed, clothed, and visited.

He was so sane he drove the neurotic leaders of the church to fury. They jumped up and down and frothed at the mouth in anger. Common people were amazed at his simplicity and understanding. Jesus knew what was in people. He exercised wisdom in his encounters with the sharp opposition. He could pinpoint a person's immediate need and speak to it with delicate precision. Jesus modeled mental health. He helped people put their identity into proper perspective. "Do not be afraid," he said on several occasions, "I have come that you might be made into a whole person."

Jesus knew what was residing in the depths of others. He not only had the ability to reveal truth, he could apply forgiveness and affirmation and introduce healing to all the resentful and twisted pieces of life. Jesus Christ was/is the epitome of human potential. The historical Jesus exuded completeness in his personhood. The early church fathers wrote, in ancient creeds, "He was very man and very God."

Today we live in a time when the pendulum is emphasizing the humanity of Jesus. People want to develop okay feelings. *Godspell, Jesus Christ Superstar,* and the whole human potential movement are signs of the times. The search for meaning is real to those of us who are lost in the crowds. We want to know who we are. We are conscious of the necessity of building creative relationships. We are committed to liberating ourselves from the bondage of tradition and long-established habits of the past. We want to be set free *to be, to do, to say.* We long for sanity in the midst of the rat race. We're hunting for a hitching post in the universe. We're questing for the very thing God wants to give each of us—abundant life. We want to live life so completely that, after we're at the other end, we can finally turn around and say, "Wow! I'm glad I came this way! Why I wouldn't have missed this trip for anything in the world!"

Jesus was also the healing listener. He never violated a single person. He was a gentleman. Yet, on the other hand, he never withheld the truth. He was full of *grace and truth.* In one sense of the word, he was so flexible and permissive that some people labeled him a loser. On the other hand, he was so unmovable that he was an enigma to those who chose to protect him. *At the same moment* he was completely in control *and* completely vulnerable!

Jesus knew himself. He knew where he came from, what he was doing, and where he was going. "Who do other men say I am?" he quizzed his learning-followers. "Oh, they say you're Elijah, or John the baptizer, or Jeremiah, or one of the prophets."

"Who do *you* think I am?" Jesus asked. Peter responded, "You're the Christ, the promised one who is to deliver your people. You are the Son of the living God."

"God has given you that perception, Simon. Remember that this insight is a gift from my Father in heaven. The human psyche cannot innately produce such spiritual perception" (paraphrase of Matthew 16:16–17).

In my personal struggle for identity I have confronted two very important questions. "Who am I?" and "Who is Jesus?"

In my quest for wholeness I've discovered that it is essential to know *whose* I am as well as *who* I am. I've noticed that I take on the characteristics of those persons to whom I entrust myself. My values, my behavior patterns, and my style of communication are shaped to some degree by the "important" people in my life. The people with whom I am most vulnerable possess a great deal of power in the intricate areas of my life. Now, if this is true, then I may be all the wiser if I anchor my vulnerability along with those whose lifestyle produces the freedom and disciplines I want to reproduce.

Our search for sanity is closely related to the people we belong to. Jesus urged us to keep on asking for sanity . . . and it will come. He said to keep on knocking . . . and not give up. God is so amazing. He has established several fail-safe systems in the universe. It's my deepest conviction that he will show up. He will not forget any of us. I may be bouncing around in the basement of utter despair, and my faith may be deadened with the impossibilities of my own sense of estrangement. But even in my despair he breaks through with a candle of hope and light. I suppose that I would never seek God if I could not experience despair. It is often my pain that wakes me up to my need for God. It may be my insanity that drives me toward the hope for sanity.

God consistently seems to teach me what I need to learn, and the history of God's action shows how impartial he is. I am convinced that he will use us if we are obedient and sensitive to his guidance. If the church is not listening, he'll use the secularist. When Jesus preached his first hometown sermon he reminded his friends of this particular truth. It infuriated the people so much they tried to push him off a high cliff. We church people may not like to admit that God can, if he so chooses, do a better job through secular unbelievers than some of us! Oftentimes we think we have a monopoly on God just because we wear his bumper stickers! Of course God is bigger than his people. And truth, I am convinced, is a gift!

So what does this mean? It helps me understand the birth of psychology, for example. Sigmund Freud, the father of modern psychology, was not a Christian. But God raised him up, and today we see the influence of "secular psychology" within the walls of the church. The human potential movement, which may look very secular and very unreligious to some of you, has been constantly chipping away at the phoniness of religiosity. God is making us more sensitive, more vulnerable, more relatable—and many of us have been influenced by this so-called secular ministry.

What if God didn't care enough to break through to you and me? We'd probably wallow around in the deserts of our own spiritual hypocrisy and never discover the land of milk and honey! Shouldn't we rather seek his forgiveness and thank him for the intelligence he shows and the depth of caring he exhibits toward us when we are so slow of heart in believing and receiving?

My initial involvement with the human potential movement was motivated by personal need, curiosity, and a willingness to discover truth and follow it's full course. Theologically I believe that Jesus was and is the truth. He embodies *all truth*. And I believe that knowing the truth does set me free. I believe that all truth leads to him, and this frees me to explore beyond the safe confines of my immediate little world.

At the same time I felt constricted in my personal relationships. I wanted to love God with abandonment. I ached to know how to communicate with clarity. Somehow I believed that God wanted me to listen to him through a secular setting. I studied the Scriptures regularly, and often I'd confront Jesus in his relationships with "worldly" people. I wanted to break out of my tight little circle. Again, God exposed me to people who introduced me to this new world of communications.

I met a psychologist and we started a group. There were nine of us—all clergy, except for the psychologist who happened to be a woman. This psychologist was devastatingly perceptive. Her catalystic technique was one of "negative caring." She cared enough to entrust the group with her anger. "You preachers make me want to vomit. You sit around with lockjaw smiles and act so ——— ——— nice. You are afraid to be yourselves."

For months I wondered if the poor devil would ever find God and get converted. I did not hear her at all. I kept smiling my inner turmoil and resentment away, and one day she tore into me. I could not admit, even to myself, my feelings of resentment. I refused to fight back. I thought of the time when I was a little boy, when Elmer tried to put my eyes out with weeds, and I didn't know how to fight back. To show anger was to violate another person. I did not know how to say "I feel hate. I feel like a trapped animal. I don't like what I hear. I don't like myself because I'm not telling you off! I feel hurt, abused, angry, exposed."

Those may have been my deeper feelings at that time but I didn't know how to cope with them until many months later. I buried the pain and stopped attending the group. Months later some of those feelings finally emerged and I understood myself a little better. I called the psychologist and made an appointment to visit with her. I told her how I felt, and to my surprise I experienced a new level of wholeness and release. My prayers were answered. I finally began to get in touch with some of the buried stuff I had blocked most of my life. But this was only a beginning, and I kept praying, "God, don't stop now! Whatever wholeness means in this particular area of my life, keep at it until you clean it all up, even if it takes more than a lifetime!"

I have habitually prayed for the healing of my memories and emotions, because I believe inward peace of mind and the healing of my emotions are closely related.

Jesus pinpointed the central dynamic of psychology when he said, "Love God with all your heart. Love your neighbor as yourself."

Here is life in a nutshell. It's up to me to crack my shell from within and discover a whole world of new treasures. When I discovered that I didn't love myself, I understood why I projected resentment and hostility on my neighbor, my wife, my children, my superiors. I was unconsciously swinging at myself and hitting them at those places where I couldn't love and accept myself.

I searched for tools so I could expose my real self to the reality of God's Love. And my search for wholeness through secular movements had a clear ring of God's guidance. Now I understand the Scripture verse, "For his sun shines on the just and the unjust," and "anyone who desires may come and drink freely from the fountain of life." God loves us all completely and he works in and through us— even when we're unaware of it!

A few years after the clergy therapy group, Betsy and I enrolled in a two week T-Group laboratory. I entered into this experience with high hopes. I wanted to be involved in a support group where deep healing could take place. I presupposed that this laboratory would equip me with new communication skills. I was not ready for what really happened.

There were ninety-eight of us and we were assigned to groups of twelve. Sensitivity trainers sat in and directed each group. We met everyday for two weeks, from eight in the morning until ten each night with an afternoon break. Our group of twelve met for the first time on Sunday afternoon at three. Twenty-four people came to our room. Our group sat on the floor in a circle, and the second group of twelve quietly observed, sitting around us in a larger circle. Two of our people started a dialogue. One person expressed what I thought was an unfair judgment regarding the other person, and I responded. "I hear what he's saying. Why are you jumping on him?" I asked, but before the fellow could come back I heard this tumultuous booming voice bellowing out, "You G__ D__ S__ O__ B__ preacher! I should have known you'd try and protect him. You're just like all the rest of 'em! You're full of s____!"

I turned around in complete astonishment. The voice belonged to my T-Group trainer. My immediate response was utter amusement. I felt no consciousness of anger. I thought of my psychologist friend in our former clergy group, and I wanted to laugh, but the atmosphere was too tense. I just sat there and blinked my eyes and waited. "What do you mean?" I asked. No answer. Days passed and I felt very much alone in the group. Sometimes I'd sit and listen without saying a word for a whole day or for two days. Whenever I related I felt put down by the group. Pangs of isolation hooked me. I had little to hold on to. I felt as though I was in between—without a grasp on the past or the future!

I expressed my feelings to the trainer, "I felt put down when you came on like that the first day. It hurt."

"Great" was his reply. That ended the ball game for me. I pulled back and did not trust him or the group anymore. The longer I sat in the group the more I felt barraged with insecurity and irregular moments of unexplainable pressure. For three days I literally doubted my own sanity!

Betsy attended another group and her experience was altogether different. Every day I longed for closing time when I could go meet her and we would go our way together and process our way through the day's experiences. I remember staying up with Betsy until two or three o'clock morning after morning, trying to work through the intricate complexities of my own shattered identity. I could not enjoy the week-end hours with the children. I completely ignored the beautiful New England countryside. I thought I was wrestling with emotional demons inside, and I threw myself at the mercy of God time and time again. "God, I've never known such pain. Don't let me go through this without your providential guidance. I'm going to fall apart if you leave me for a moment. I feel paralyzed and numb. Help me!"

This continued until two days before the two-week session was over. I desperately wanted the acceptance of the group, but I did not know how to ask for it. I guess I was too stubborn to ask them for what I needed most, so I kept it all in. I didn't think they'd understand if I told them. I was afraid they'd belittle me so I held it all in! I really don't think they knew I was in such pain. I was too insecure to tell them. I never did.

Finally, two days before the end of the session, the T-Group trainer suggested that the group accept Hal, "just as he is." I wanted to believe it but it came off so phony. I just wanted to get away. I tried to come back "into the group" several times, but I was so insecure I never communicated what I really felt inside. They could see my mask, and they rejected it, but they could not see my pain. I got into my car and spent my hour of free time alone. I drove off the road and followed a little path back into the woods. It turned out to be a garbage dump. I sat there on the garbage dump and cried and prayed. In exasperated whispers I said, "God, I can't take it anymore. I'm hurting so deeply, and I don't know what to do about it. I need help! Please . . . please do something for me."

I had only a few minutes to get back to the group. I thought about how beautifully Betsy related to me. Day after day she stayed with me, listening and encouraging me along. I thought about the children and the great time they were having a couple of miles away. I looked through the trees and for the first time in a week or more, I felt the warmth of the sun! And then it happened. I was completely surprised by what seemed to be a single moment of overwhelming joy! The heaviness lifted. The pain went away. The trees and the lake and the sky moved and danced and I settled into a long-awaited peacefulness. I breathed deeply. Something quiet and real clicked inside. To this day I can't explain what happened. All I know is that I got in the car and left the garbage behind!

I went back to the group and had a ball! They seemed different, somehow. I felt self-acceptance and was released in the process. They

SOMETHING'S HAPPENED TO ME

were free to feel whatever they wanted to feel about me. I think some of them knew something had happened to me. At any rate, I had a new self-image and it was for real. I felt put together. I felt absolutely sane!

Somehow, Jesus had once again touched my life in an unusual way and extended to me the gift of wholeness.

Jesus, I feel like a guy who said, "I really can't explain it. All I can say is once I was blind. Now I can see."

I can't explain the full meaning of my growth . . . or the love that sometimes surges up inside during those great moments of healing and wonderment. I know that I enjoy those moments more than the times when I'm down and out and unable to cope. But aren't both part of growing up?

All I can say is thanks! Thanks for being too real to explain or describe. Thanks for the experience that speaks for itself. . . .

Jesus Christ, you are the reason I can experience sanity. You are reality incarnate. You are the center of awareness in my universe. My world works when you are my hitching post. Jesus, you are Lord indeed! Out of my need I'm discovering your Lordship, and out of your Lordship I'm celebrating my own identity.

18

I've Fallen
in Love
Again!

1. What did you want most from your parents? Did you receive it? What does that say about the way you relate today? Did you misinterpret any signals of parental love? How did your parents show you their love?

2. What's one of the most significant encounters you ever experienced with your parents in terms of a healing relationship? When did it happen? How do you feel about it now?

3. How do you feel about the church today? With your own personhood? The Bible? your past? The world of nature about you? Your family? Where do you feel most loved and alive?

4. As you remember back into your unique history, what are the major events and strands that seem to tie your search for wholeness into focus? Do you see your behavior in the past as symbols of searching? Has this book helped you become more aware of your past? Your potential? How?

18

I've Fallen in Love Again!

John 5:6—*Do you really want to be made whole?*
John 14:25–26—*Who will lead us towards wholeness?*
Romans 3:11—*What is God's gift to the person who searches for wholeness?*
Ephesians 5:15—*What is my responsibility now that I am called to receive the undeserved gift of God's love?*

I knew I had somehow misread my mother's signals, and I wanted to work through my relationship with her. I wanted this trip to be different. "Honey," I said to Betsy, "it's time I consciously tried to understand my mother as a person. All my life I've been expecting her to be someone other than who she really is. I've carried resentment in my heart for years. I've been terribly unfair to her and I want this trip to be providential for us. Let's agree together in prayer that God will teach me the lessons I need to learn on this trip."

I was thirty-four years old at the time. I tried to concentrate on what it would mean to develop a new relationship with my mother. At that time I lived in Southern California and she lived in North Carolina. I looked out the window of the big jet and prayed, "God, give me a handle. Where do I begin?" And this thought came, "Why not give her what you want most from her? Maybe she's starving for the same thing!"

"Lord," I continued, "I don't even know what I want most from her. What do I want?"

I meditated and soon it became as clear as day. I thought back to my early childhood. I was the first of four boys. By the time I was old enough to know my name, Kemp was born. Then Tom. By the time Bill was born, my parents were too busy trying to keep the bare essentials together. I think I felt cheated, and I wanted more affirmation and time with my mother. I wanted her to play with me and hug me and tell me who I was. I wanted her to snuggle and hold me close. Finally, at thirty-four years of age (and after having four children of my own) it dawned on me!

"Why, I'll never be *enough* to my four children and I'm sure they must feel cheated at times. Even if I gave them all I'm humanly capable of giving, it would never be enough. Now I understand something of what my mother was going through."

I decided I'd kiss her and hug her and tell her how good it was to be with her. During that visit I asked new questions and learned a lot about my mother's childhood. I learned, for example, that her father died when she was a very young child. Somehow I never thought about how his death cheated her from a lot of cuddling! She and I talked about my childhood. Her feelings about me did not coincide with my fantasies. What I thought she felt was not very accurate. I continued to ask questions I never dared ask before. Again I heard new sounds and gained new insights about myself and my childhood memories.

"You were loved very deeply," she assured me. "I kept at you, not because I didn't like you, but because I wanted you to make something of yourself. I didn't want you boys to grow up without goals and disciplines. My dream for you, and for all the other boys, has always been that you go out from here and be somebody you can be proud of. If I pushed you too hard, it was because I felt you needed to be disciplined. I wanted you to know the importance of finishing a job . . . of being on time. That's why I *sounded* like a crab, and that's why you may have felt rejection from me. It was because I did care enough to stay with you when you wanted to quit."

I knew every word she uttered was gold-plated reality. I felt my heart filling up with joy and deep appreciation for her. I felt a releasing sensation. What a risk she took, I thought, when she tried to harness my unwieldy, rebellious, strong will!

For the first time in my life it became clear to me. My mother loved me with tough love. She was not permissive. She dared to discipline and challenge me to higher things. I *thought* she didn't like me the way I was. I *thought* I had to accomplish something great so she'd like me. I misunderstood her intentions all these years! I was loved and affirmed, and my mother consistently gave me the very best she had to give! Now, years later, I see what I could not see then.

I SEE IT WITH NEW EYES

A whole new world of possibilities opened as a result of this encounter. I thanked God for giving me the opportunity to communicate
with my mother. Since that time she has become a very real person to me. I had blocked her out for so long. I guess the best way
to describe what happened between us is to say that I've fallen in
love with a very special human being.

I had more homework to do during that same visit. My maternal
grandmother and I talked about my childhood. I thanked her for
making me do my chores until they were all completed. We chatted
about the times we worked in the garden and fed the chickens. She
told me about her childhood and her relationship to her parents. I
put a few more important pieces of the puzzle together. As she talked
about her past I understood even more about my mother.

Things seem different now when I visit the house in which I was
born. We all seem to be more relaxed. We know we've worked
through to each other. I've fallen in love with my people on a deeper
level! I've learned that my parents and grandparents gave me more

than I ever consciously knew at that time. During my childhood years and adolescence I wanted them to be something other than who they were, and I failed many times to enjoy and understand them as they were. Thus, there was resentment. I was blinded by my own inability to read through to their humanity. The more I become aware of myself as an adult the more I am capable of reaching back into my past and uncovering those memories. I was isolating myself by my controlling, self-centered attitudes. Now I see how patient, how loving, how responsible, and how committed they were to me—especially when I did not know it. Today I am overwhelmed with gratitude and amazement.

My Christian pilgrimage is divided into segments of experiments . . . lots of mistakes . . . thousands. But I'm hopeful that they aren't wasted mistakes. I'm convinced that God also makes himself known through weakness, failure, and mistakes. Whenever I've hurt enough or felt secure enough to peek from behind my mask and know a little more about the dynamics of my own uniqueness, I encounter the consistency and the availability of the grace of God through some timely soul nearby.

We all try desperately hard to find the pot of gold at the end of the rainbow. I'm convinced that each of us wants wholeness and sanity more than anything. We are all searching, struggling towards what we hope will turn out to be all we expected. We try to get there by working hard, by having fun, by introspection, by serving, by communicating, by analysis, and a thousand other ways. We are all, I suppose, "gutting it out" one way or another.

The miracle is, God knows our needs and he relates to them and sets us free to love with tremendous abandonment. We look around in amazement at what we're able to enjoy!

I've fallen in love with the church. I no longer expect perfection from her. I realize that she is full of people like myself—people who struggle and grope for love and meaning. People who need grace.

I've fallen in love with the person I am at this moment. Perhaps this is the greatest miracle of all, because the person I am is not all he shall be. I'm beginning to celebrate my limitations as well as my gifts. I am delighted that I am able to grow and understand more about myself.

I've fallen in love with the Bible. There's a new reason to read the Scriptures. I'm so glad I memorized a few verses years ago, even if I memorized them for the wrong reasons! Today those verses serve me well. Quite often I find it very helpful to read and then brood over certain verses. Sometimes I paraphrase them and type them on cards and read them on the way to work.

I've fallen in love with my past. For so many years I could not accept my past. I thought my past was my number one enemy! I misread the script completely! It took me over thirty-four years to discover the simple fact that every person's past is sacred once he accepts it and learns from it.

I've fallen in love with nature. Flowers do have texture and color and life! Simple things like driftwood, swaying trees, and butterflies bring joy, and sometimes tears. I feel a kinship to the world all around me.

I've fallen in love with my family. I love to be at home and watch the children play and run through the house. The best part of any day for me is after supper. On a typical summer day we get on our bikes and ride over to the playground. We all become children. Then, after the kids are tucked away, Betsy and I enjoy those sacred uninterrupted moments of sharing the day's feelings. Sometimes that's rather hard. Sometimes we are captured by sheer joy. Quite often we pray together before we fall asleep.

I've fallen in love with my growing edge. I'm glad I own my particular set of problems. Somehow God has blessed each of us with the raw material necessary for eventual maturity. Without my set of problems I could not grow properly. So, in Jesus' name, I embrace my humanity. I need my set of challenges so I can continue growing toward the person I hope to become. I will fight and resist from time to time, but deep down I'm aware that healing and wholeness cannot come unless I let God take me through those painful places.

Several years ago I had a chat with a very wise old gentleman. We were talking about what it means to be a Christian. "What does it mean to be converted?" I quizzed him.

"I don't think a person is genuinely converted unless he is converted out of a response to God's love. God accepts us because he loves us. We are changed because we are loved," my friend said.

I think the greatest gift God gives to you and me is the gift of responding to his love! I'm not sure I understand what that means. I am sure it'll take at least one lifetime to catch a glimpse of all he has in store for us!

I am now quite certain that God's nature is love. All that he does is directed by his love. Even his anger. God, the Father of our Lord Jesus, is very dependable. When everything else fails he remains unchangeable. That's great to know! You see, I need to know that

HELP ME UNWRAP MY GIFT

every day! Every day I need to know, to experience, God's forgiveness, acceptance, and love. I've discovered that I can know this by faith—and it really works!

As I remember back over my past and peek into the portholes of my search for wholeness I perceive that I'm not as perfect as I wanted to be, but I'm more whole than I ever anticipated. I think I'm learning the difference between perfection and wholeness. One is sought for through performance; the other is a gift. For the most of my life I tried to be perfect, thinking I should be.

That's why I followed my heroes around. That's why I tried so hard to be something I could never be. That's why my life is bombarded with countless vignettes of imperfect performances. I searched for wholeness with the wrong priorities. I thought I had to do it on my own.

Even through the confusion and conflict God is helping me depend more on him and less upon my human resources. I'm not quite as uptight about being a performer, even though I forget it time and time again. I guess I'll always struggle with this. Even so, nothing's lost. God can use everything to bring me towards wholeness. He can even use my imperfection!

Jesus, I do want to be made whole! I'm ready to get up off my pallet and walk—even if my wholeness means confusion and conflict to others.

I don't know what wholeness means, except I think it means that things come together. I want the rest of my life to be the very best, and I want you to make me accountable in my journey towards wholeness.

Somehow I believe that you are eternally concerned for each of us, and your gift of wholeness will help us grow more to be like our true selves. Isn't that true?

Jesus, thank you for releasing us to know that perfection and wholeness aren't the same. Thank you for the gift we'll never earn, and for the joy of growing and changing every day.

Thank you, also, that none of us has to grow alone. We can walk towards wholeness together and celebrate your body.

PROPERTY OF
LIVING FAITH CENTER
LIBRARY
SANTA BARBARA, CA